A
Pathway
To
Permanent Peace:

A Ten-Stop Spiritual Marathon

(Volume 5 of the "Step-By-Step" Bible study series)

by

Bruce Leiter

published author of both fiction and
nonfiction

<u>Also by the author (these books plus one at
Amazon.com)</u>:

Doubtbusters! God Is My Shrink! (a
postmodern *Mere Christianity* and a
model for personal outreach—the
author as a friend with two fictional
skeptics)

Be Bolder Growin' Older (a devotional
Bible study preparing people to

experience Jesus' victory for the losses and changes of old age)

Pray and Play: Dealing with a Fun-Loving Culture (a devotional Bible study helping people have God-honoring fun)

Divided Together 2084 (a fictional mystery novel with a Muslim, Akilah, and a Christian, Farhan, fighting serial killers and terrorists in a Muslim land and discussing their differing beliefs—also as an audiobook narrated by the author on Audible, coming soon)

Divided Together 2094 (a fictional mystery novel in which Farhan and his family move back to the States (Indianapolis); and, since the USA has become mostly atheist, he teams up with an atheist to fight three kinds of violent crimes, has discussions about belief and unbelief, and teaches at the local university—also in Kindle. It is the 2nd in the Farhan Trilogy)

Divided Together 2104 (the 3rd in the
Farhan mystery trilogy in which he
teams up with a Hindu to investigate
"white-collar crimes" by scam artists
stealing from people, while they
discuss their differing beliefs)

*News Tries to Control You: Be Equipped to
Evaluate It* (a nonfiction book that
helps you sort the media bias from
your news sources—written during a
few days at the end of September in
the heat of the 2020 election season)

*Overcome Modern Idols: Beat Thirty-one
False Gods* (a devotional Bible study
for individuals and groups,
equipping you with the Bible's
teachings about the false gods of our
age and the way you can defeat them)

<u>**A Must Pre-Read: Seven Essential Tips for Reading This Book**</u>

What is the need for this book? The full title of this book is A *Pathway to Permanent Peace: A Ten-Stop Marathon.* The questions arise, "Why do we need a book about getting peace instead of anger and anxiety? Isn't it okay to worry and get angry once in a while?" We only need to be aware of our world's rage expressed in terrorism and mass murder to see the results of destructive anger. Less destructive anger at the very least creates barriers between us and others. Also, anxiety can hurt our interactions with other people and keep us from productive activity for Jesus. I'll deal with the answers to these questions in more detail in this book, but I'll say here that if you want to be free from self-centered anxiety and anger, God has revealed the way to his emotion-solution in the Bible.

This book, the fourth in the "Step-By-Step Series" of devotional Bible studies, provides for you a step-by-step journey toward having on-going inner peace. The first three books are *Be Bolder Growin' Older, Pray and Play, Overcome Modern Idols: Beat Thirty-one False Gods,* and *Overcome Secular Humanism.* See my website, www.growingtoknowGod.org for more information.

Where did the idea for this book come from? The background for this book comes from the repression of my anger and anxiety about my losses and other people's unloving actions that were buried in my unconscious mind for the first forty-three years of my life, twenty-seven of those years as a Christian. Some of those experiences I will describe in this book. God used psychological means and his inspired Word to enable me to get in touch with the anger and anxiety that were present in my emotional life but of which I was unaware. Then, he used a biblical pattern to decrease my anger and anxiety dramatically, as I will explain. During the last years of my life (more than three decades), I have meditated on this subject and tried to put God's Word into practice by his grace and love alone.

What is the "Step-By-Step Series"? As the first page says, this book is volume five of the "Step-By-Step Series." As I said above, the first volume is *Be Bolder Growin' Older*, published by CrossLink Publishing, which prepares younger and middle-age people for growing older and enables older people to find Jesus' victory during that life-stage. The second book's full title is *Pray and Play: Dealing With a Fun-Loving Culture*, which helps readers do God-centered fun. The third one is *Overcome Modern Idols: Beat 31 False gods,* while the fourth one is *Overcome Secular Humanism.*

The whole series, which I hope will have many volumes, invites readers on a step-by-step journey with Jesus in reading and discussing the Bible as our divine Rescuer's Tourist Guide toward the goals of spiritual maturity and final perfection. It also deals with the many contrasts in the Bible that may seem to contradict each other but really don't—like finding on-going peace about the losses and challenges of life even though those events do not change.

Individual readers can read all of the books in the "Step-By-Step Series" for their devotions and personal benefit, but I also designed the books with discussion questions for group discussion before each step of practical application. As a result, each book is useful for both personal and group study as a devotional Bible study.

What is this Bible study about?
Marathon runners in outside marathons
benefit from stopping at many refreshment
stations along their route. Some American
marathons call them fluid-stations, but
marathons in other countries call them
refreshment stations. The latter seemed more
appropriate to my book's purpose, because
the Holy Spirit is God the Father's direct
means through Jesus' victory to refresh our
life's journey spiritually. In this book, you
have ten refreshment stations symbolizing the
Holy Spirit's use of God's Word to help our
spiritual health.

In addition to the ten-refreshment-station
process in this book, you will encounter
several other steps of practical application in
all of the books that will help you put the
Bible into daily practice on your Jesus-led
trip.

Where is our journey with Jesus going?
In this book, our terrific tourist trip with our
right Ruler-Guide follows Paul's path in
Philippians 3:10-14, where he uses running
words from the Greek Olympic Games to
describe our race toward our future
resurrection perfection that he will give us at
Jesus' return. Then, he will give our lives

permanent, perfect peace with final flawlessness in his new creation. The writer to the Hebrews also describes that race in Hebrews 12:1, 2. We run only in Jesus' strength with spiritual progress in this life and the goal of final perfection when we enter the next one.

How can I get peace in this life? Of course, you need to read and gain refreshment from the stations and application steps in this book to receive God's gift of inner peace, which is different from human peace. He wants to give us emotional progress in this life as well as perfect, eternal peace when Jesus returns. Therefore, you can find peace by following his peace path as described in this book from his inspired Book, regardless of your circumstances.

How easy is the peace process? On the one hand, it's easy for you because only God's victorious power through Jesus changes us, not our own strength or will power. Also, only in his power through Jesus' all-powerful victory can we finish the marathon and gain God's great peace. In other words, running this marathon is easy only through Jesus' divine, unlimited power that he wants to give believers.

On the other hand, investigating our emotions of anger and anxiety is not easy to do. However, I believe from experience that it's better to face our emotional "demons" than to let them increase in our unconscious minds, because anger and anxiety always have a way of surfacing and hurting us and other people.

Please read (and discuss) my book and follow all ten of the refreshment stations in our spiritual marathon persistently along with meditating on and putting the Bible passages into practice. May the only-true God of the Bible abundantly bless your emotional journey with Jesus, dear reader!

Table of Contents

Refreshment Station 3: Understand the conscious, subconscious, and unconscious minds

Refreshment Station 4: Get in touch with your anger and anxiety

Refreshment Station 5: Acknowledge your grief

Life's Emotional Marathon Part III: Pursue a prayerful Pathway to peace (outer and inner—Rom. 5:1-4; Phil. 4:6, 7)

Refreshment Station 6: Understand your anger and depression

Refreshment Station 7: Experience tears and hope

Refreshment Station 8: Do a different kind of praying (6 kinds [praise, thanks, confession, prayer for others and ourselves, and lamenting]—two kinds of complaining in the Bible)

A. Unbelievers' complaining

B. Believers' complaining

**Life's Emotional Marathon Part I**:
Understand divine emotions.

I've never run a marathon, but I contend that our lives are like marathon races. It's a mystery to me how a person can run twenty-six-plus miles. I know that it takes a lot of training, but training wouldn't help me run that far. I prefer swimming a half-hour at local indoor pools, an activity my doctor says is "very good exercise." Anyway, a number of marathons (mostly outside the States) have "refreshment stations" every mile or so to help people re-hydrate to avoid cramping up. For me, those stations would prevent me from dying, if I arrived at any of them! I'm sure that my body would complain loudly long before the first station.

At some marathons, fluid-stations provide water or one of the power drinks all along the way and some food later in the race to help sustain runners' health.

The Christian life is like running a marathon, and Jesus provides "refreshment stations" along the way as the Holy Spirit refreshes our spiritual health so that we can be his agents of blessing to people around us. Listen to him in John 7:37-39: "On the last and greatest day of the Feast, Jesus stood and said in a loud voice, 'If anyone is thirsty, let him come to me and drink. Whoever believes in me, as the Scriptures have said, streams of living water will flow from within him.' [Then, John comments,] By this he meant the Spirit, whom those who believed in him were later to receive."

Notice that John, under God's inspiration, interprets Jesus' reference to the living water as the Holy Spirit. As our life's marathon proceeds, God the Father gives us the Holy Spirit at our refreshment stations through Jesus' victory to strengthen us as we run our race. At the ten refreshment stations in this book, the 3-in-1 God wants to empower our emotions to give us his amazing peace at the end of this part of our life's race. I invite you, dear reader, to persevere in running your emotional marathon to gain each of the ten refreshment stations in order to finish the race. Like a marathon, the race is very hard at times, but God's peace awaits you at the finish-line!

You'll notice that Part I involves understanding God's emotions. Many people and groups in our world deny for a variety of reasons that God has emotions. However, the Bible doesn't mince words in making the claim that God has emotions. You would have to delete many verses in the Bible to take out all of the references to God's emotions.

However, his emotions are different from ours in that his feelings are defect-free, whereas ours are far from perfect.

First, before we investigate those verses, we must understand that God's feelings are not self-centered. For example, he is not vengeful in response to human rebellion by seeking petty revenge. Instead, he is long-suffering and patient, unlike most humans.

Second, the Bible's writers did not invent God to be like humans. Instead, he inspired the Bible to describe his creation of humanity in Genesis 1:27, "So God created man in his own image, in the image of God he created him; male and female he created them." God created us to be like him in some ways, not the other way around. The humans who wrote the Bible definitely did not imagine him to be a larger-than-life human.

The God of the Bible is unlike the gods of the other nations around the biblical writers' Israel, since all of those gods were larger-than-life super-humans with many self-centered human qualities. Instead, the God of the Bible is all-powerful, all-knowing, everywhere-present, and eternal—all decidedly non-human qualities. He is also full of grace, love, and mercy, while at the same time having perfect qualities of justice, holiness, and righteousness. He is our Creator-Rescuer. Therefore, as our Maker, he is also our rightful Judge, who expects us to follow his will as revealed in his Word, the Bible. Thus, his anger expresses his perfect justice in punishing human rebellion against his laws that are for our good.

Refreshment Station 1: Understand God's perfect power and justice...in punishing unbelievers

God the Judge's perfectly-just anger in Moses' writings

Our first marathon refreshment station from God is his provision of the Holy Spirit so that we can understand his anger. Yes, God feels anger. I'm afraid that the preaching pendulum in many Christian churches has swung from a century or two of messages like Jonathan Edwards' sermon "Sinners in the Hands of an Angry God," which God used to spark the first American revival. Generations of churchgoers heard about God as our just Judge condemning sinners to hell.

While those messages were true, such preachers' almost-constant emphasis on God's anger at sinners seems to have caused the present swing away from God's justice to his love and grace. Why can't we find a happy medium and emphasize both God's anger and his love, which both take centerstage in his inspired Book.

However, in order to receive God's inner peace, we must understand again God's perfectly just divine nature.

For example, when we read the Book of Numbers, the fourth of the five books of Moses, God has already sent ten miraculous plagues to the Egyptians, who have refused to release their Israelite slaves; raised the water of the Red Sea in walls to let the Israelites go through the sea on dry land to escape their unjust slavery; drowned the stubbornly-self-centered Egyptians in the same Red Sea; miraculously provided water from a desert rock and an amazing, miraculous "bread" (manna) that has supplied their physical needs; spoken the Ten Commandments with his own voice; provided for them a place of worship, the Tabernacle; given them his many right rules for their thankful living; and gone in front of them in a cloudy pillar by day and a fiery one at night.

Even after all that evidence that he is with them and that he will take care of them as his people, Moses writes in Numbers 11:1, "Now, the people complained about their hardships in the hearing of the LORD, and when he heard them, his anger was aroused. Then fire from the LORD burned among them and consumed some of the outskirts of the camp. When the people cried out to Moses, he prayed to the LORD and the fire died down." God is rightly angry at his people's complaining to Moses, not God, in unbelief because they don't have any meat to eat. Manna was his bread for their lives, looking forward to Jesus, the "bread of life" (John 6).

In response to Israel's complaining in unbelief, God certainly can wipe them out of existence completely. In fact, if we were God, we humans would have destroyed the Israelites completely long before this point, for example, when they whined with their backs trapped against the Red Sea and the Egyptian army closing in on them. However, at this time, God's fire blackens their camp's outskirts as God's warning to them that his right, patient anger has its limits.

People often rail at God when they suffer and turn away from him in unbelief. Such is the case with Israel, only because they miss the meat of Egypt. They have selective memories, since they conveniently forget that they have groaned to God about their cruel Egyptian slavery.

However, Moses shows a different kind of complaining in part of the same chapter, Numbers 11:10-15. In response to the people's grumbling in unbelief about God's gift of the miraculous manna, "the LORD became exceedingly angry, and Moses was troubled" (verse 10b). The Israelites, by and large, throw an unbelieving pity-party, while Moses throws a believing pity-party.

In essence, Moses asks why God has put the exceedingly-heavy burden of Israel on his eighty-year-old shoulders to carry them to the Promised Land. God responds lovingly to Moses' believing pity-party by having him choose seventy elders in Israel to judge smaller disputes in order to ease Moses' judicial burden (verses 16, 17). A significant detail in Moses' inspired narrative is Numbers 11:25, "Then the LORD came down in the cloud and spoke with him, and he took of the Spirit that was on him and put the Spirit on the seventy elders," who then prophesy only once.

As with Moses, God always responds to us in love when we share our anger and anxiety with him in faith, as we will see in much more detail later in our study.

On the other hand, in response to the people's unbelieving pity-party, the LORD promises and then sends to the people a huge flock of quail that are a yard deep on the ground for a day's walk in all directions. They greedily gorge themselves on the quail. However, "before it could be consumed, the anger of the LORD burned against the people, and he struck them with a severe plague" (verses 31-34).

At another refreshment station, we will learn more about how to complain in faith to God like Moses as part of the pathway to peace. However, here we notice that God has the emotion of anger but that it is a just and perfect anger unlike Israel's self-centered anger in the desert.

God's emotions in the Bible's historical and wisdom books

One assumption in the whole Bible is that God is our just Judge. After all, the Bible also assumes that he has created us and therefore has the right to require our obedience to his will as revealed in his Word, the Bible.

For example, Psalm 75 clearly quotes God as saying, "I choose the appointed time; it is I who judge uprightly" (verse 2). Then, the psalmist observes, "But it is God who judges. He brings one down, he exalts another" (verse 7).

Moreover, Solomon prays to God at the temple dedication, "When a man wrongs his neighbor and is required to take an oath and he comes and swears the oath before your altar in the temple, then hear from heaven and act. Judge between your servants, condemning the guilty and bringing down on his own head what he has done. Declare the innocent not guilty and so establish his innocence" (1 Kings 8:31, 32). Here,

Solomon rightly balances God's just anger, love, and grace in freely accepting believers.

In spite of people's denials of God's just anger at human injustice, most of us want justice in the world. The Bible clearly describes God our Judge's just anger in declaring people guilty or not guilty.

Thus, the next step is to understand the Bible's clear teaching that hell, as a place of sad separation from God, is the expression of his just anger against humans' ready rebellion during their whole lives, when they have freely chosen to be separate from him. During that time, he is incredibly patient with their many sins.

However, when they die and go to hell, he lets them have their wish to leave God out of their lives without the false god-substitutes they have had in this life.

Also, when King Rehoboam, Solomon's son, is king of Judah, he and the people desert God's law (2 Chron.12:1-11). As we see many times throughout the Old Testament, the vicious sin-cycle is that Israel strays from God's rules, he permits them to experience disaster and distress, and they turn back to him. Then, they wander from his ways and again experience his just anger and his loving rescue.

In the case of Rehoboam's Judah, God sends the Egyptian King Shishak to attack and take over the land. Then the LORD sends Prophet Shemaiah to say to the leaders, "This is what the LORD says, 'You have abandoned me; therefore, I abandon you to Shishak.' The leaders of Israel and the king humbled themselves and said, 'The LORD is just.'" (verse 5b-6).

God's compassionate response to Israel's repentance is to show his love instead of his just anger by rescuing them from Shishak's destruction. However, he does say through the prophet, "My wrath will not be poured out on Jerusalem through Shishak. They will, however, become subject to him so that they may learn the difference between serving me and the kings of other lands'" (verses 7c-8). God's discipline for his repentant people is an expression of his tough love, whereas when unbelievers rebel in disobedience, his anger falls on them, resulting in his punishment.

Thus, we see throughout God's inspired Word that he is both justly angry and amazingly loving. He shows one or the other emotion depending on humans' actions. He has every right to kill us in our mothers' wombs because of our innate rejection of him and his will, but he allows most of us to be born and allows us to go on our self-centered ways. In addition, he blesses his created beings with life, health, and abilities to do many actions, even though we choose selfishly without our focus on him. Instead, we are born to ready rebellion or passive resistance unless he intervenes to deliver us through Jesus' perfect actions and the Holy Spirit's miracles in our lives.

In Psalm 10, the unnamed psalmist describes an evil person's complete disobedience to God in his cruel actions toward his helpless victims (verses 2-11). In verses 1 and 12-18, the writer calls on the God of perfect justice to defend the victimized: "Why, O LORD, do you stand far off? Why do you hide yourself in times of trouble? ... Arise, LORD. Lift up you hand, O God. Do not forget the helpless.... But you, O God, do see trouble and grief; you consider it to take it in hand.... Break the arm of the wicked and evil man; call him to account for his wickedness that would not be found out. The LORD is King for ever and ever" (verses 1, 12, 14a, 15-16a).

The inspired psalmist assumes that our divine Judge has standards and that people who violate those rules will receive his just punishment. God always has fully gracious love and completely just anger. The writer appeals like a legal prosecutor to the just Judge to right the wrongs done by ungodly humans.

In many such psalms in which the writer pleads for God to punish evil people, you might picture him as the prosecutor in a courtroom pleading the case against the defendant before the Judge of the universe.

Furthermore, the Bible makes clear that we have all violated God's will. We stand before our Judge guilty as charged unless someone takes our place in taking on himself our just punishment. If we accept Jesus' death in our place as God's willing, provided Substitute, God's right anger against our passive and outright rebellion has punished him in our place.

As I write these words, news accounts are describing the Islamic State's cruel wickedness in terrorist violence that has caused three hundred fifty-five mass shootings this year alone in the United States. The Paris and San Bernardino massacres by Muslim terrorists dedicated to the Islamic State make me yearn for Jesus' Second Coming, when the Day of Judgment will bring his just anger to a final conclusion, sadly, in hell for unrepentant people's lives. That result would have been mine except for Jesus' suffering and death on a criminal's cross. That torture instrument also reveals, in a deeper way, God's expression of both his perfect love and his anger.

At this point, it's appropriate for me to note that the writer of Psalm 96 calls us to rejoice because God "comes to judge the earth. He will judge the world in righteousness and the peoples in his truth" (verse 13). See also Psalm 99. The only way we can rejoice about his judgment is if we throw our lives on his mercy and, at the same time, claim Jesus' triumph for our rescue from his rightful wrath.

Bible Discussion Questions:

1. How is the Christian life like running a marathon? Explain your reaction to the author's use of ten refreshment stations like those that help runners on a marathon course. What is the meaning of the symbolism of the author's "stations"? Explain.

2. Why do you suppose unbelieving people live selfish lives rather than seeking God's will? What does the Bible say about unbelieving selfishness? Why?

3. What is your reaction to the Bible passages' descriptions of God's anger? Why do you feel that way?

4. Read Numbers 11. What are God's different reactions to Israel's and Moses' complaints? Why does he react so differently? Explain.

5. Read 2 Chronicles 12:1-11. Why does God let the Egyptian King Shishak rule over repentant Israel, according to verse 8? Explain his reason. In the light of this verse, why do you think he lets us suffer? (See also 2 Corinthians 12:1-10 for Paul's "thorn in the flesh.")

6. Read Psalms 10, 75, and 96. What does the idea of a king mean to you? How do kings rule in the ancient world? How was their rule different from the way Queen Elizabeth of England does today? Explain. What does the Bible's description of God's rule say about God and our daily lives as Christians? Why?

7. What new ideas have you learned in this book's first part? What made them new to you? Why?

* * *

One Step On Our Journey With Jesus: If you have had any wrong ideas about God's emotions and rule of the world, confess those misconceptions to God and ask him to replace them with the truths of the Bible. Then, praise him for his perfect emotions and rule of his creation.

* * *

God's amazing divine nature

Many people have imagined that God is a Santa in the sky giving us gifts because our lives are more good than bad. The writer of Psalm 139 gives us an awesome picture of our amazing God. In the psalm's prayer format, the psalmist says that God knows him inside and out (verses 1-5), is everywhere (verses 6-12), has created him in his mother's womb (verses 13-16a), has planned all of his days (verse 16b), and has countless thoughts (verses 17, 18). He also calls on God to judge wicked people (verses 19-22), search him thoroughly to discover his sins (verse 23, 24a), and lead him in correct ways (verse 24b).

God has inspired the Bible's writer of Psalm 139 to tell us what he is like. In that amazing psalm, he says that God is all-knowing, present everywhere, and all-powerful in creating all humans. He also guides all his humans' lives and has unlimited thinking abilities. The psalmist also claims that God is the perfect Judge with perfect anger toward imperfect people (all of us) and that he rescues believers with his undeserved love to guide them to do his will. Why don't we praise the LORD for his amazing divine nature and also submit to his will?

In another passage, Lamentations 3:55-66, Jeremiah praises God for his rescue as his all-seeing Deliverer (verses 55-60). But he also calls on God as the just Judge to provide him with justice against his enemies (verses 61-66). One cannot escape the conclusion from all of the Old Testament that the LORD (Yahweh) knows all human thoughts, decisions, feelings, and actions. He also shows all humanity his perfect justice to pronounce unrepentant sinners, guilty, and repentant sinner-saints, not guilty.

What a comfort it is that God will administer his justice to all stubborn rebels against his rule and give his loving forgiveness to committed believers like Jeremiah. Come soon, Lord Jesus!

So that we don't think that only the Old Testament describes the God of justice, as some people have thought, let's look at 2 Corinthians 5:1-10. In the first nine verses, Paul writes that he longs to have the "out-of-body" experience of death when he would be with the Lord Jesus. Instead, while he waits for his death, his goal (and ours) is to please God whether we are alive or dead. In this passage, Paul clearly teaches that when we believers die, our souls or lives go out of our dead bodies to be with Jesus. They do not "sleep," cease to exist, or get reincarnated in another body, as many people teach.

Then, Paul goes on to write, "For we must all appear before the judgment seat of Christ, that each one may receive what is due him for the things done while in the body whether good or bad." If you know anything about Paul's inspired writings, he does not teach here that our actions gain Jesus' guilty or not-guilty verdict.

Instead, he says that our actions in this life will determine our reward in the next life. Both our actions and rewards are gifts of God's grace and are all to his credit. They are nothing to make us proud of ourselves.

However, the God-man Jesus will judge all people when he returns. That final day comforts me greatly because Jesus will call all people to account for their unloving actions. Jesus will judge both terrorists and hypocrites rightly.

God's just punishment of unbelievers

When I read the Muslims' holy book, the Qur'an, for research, I was struck with the fact that about every other page, Allah threatens that for the reader's unbelief and disobedience, he will send that person to hell. One passage depicts the good angels laughing as they pour scalding water on people in hell. I don't believe in such a God, but Muslims have a right to believe in one, if they wish.

An opposite idea that many people have is that hell doesn't exist. After all, they say, how can a loving God banish anyone to such a horrible place? Such people base their statement on their human reasoning rather than on God's Word, the Bible.

I respond that, yes, the true God is loving, but he also shows his justice, since he is all people's rightful Creator and Judge. However, the Bible does not contain a belief system of fear of God's punishment unlike other religions. For example, Moses in Deuteronomy 6:5-6 makes clear a truth that the whole Bible repeats often. It is that our faith response to God's will must be grateful love, not slavish fear, "Hear, O Israel: The LORD our God, the LORD is one. Love the LORD your God with all your heart and with all your soul and with all your strength."

Furthermore, Leviticus 19:18 adds the other great commandment, according to Jesus, "Do not seek revenge or bear a grudge against one of your people, but love your neighbor as yourself. I am the LORD."

On the other hand, Deuteronomy 29:19-29 describes the case of a hypocritical Israelite who calls a blessing on himself and, as a result, thinks that he is safe even though he has no intention of following the true God. In Israel, such a hypocrite can, by himself, bring God's curse on the land (verse 19).

A parallel example today would be a person who joins a church because such a membership would be good for his business, not because he loves Jesus. The result may be that God might withdraw his blessing from that church, because they do not rightly examine and teach that new member.

Moses goes on to describe God's reaction to such hypocrites, "The LORD will never be willing to forgive him; his wrath and zeal will burn against that man. All of the curses written in this book will fall upon him, and the LORD will blot out his name from under heaven" (verse 20). Notice that God's diligent wrath or anger results when people merely pretend to be true believers. How much more do we call down on ourselves God's anger when we sin publicly or privately in rebellion against him!

Of course, I need to point out that Jesus' death on the cross does away with the Old Testament law's outward form concerning Israel's life in the Promised Land. Moses' words are in the context of his giving Israel's national law governing the people's largely outward conduct. On the other hand, the principle of God's anger against disobedience to God's will carries over to the New Testament, as we will see.

Later in Deuteronomy 29, Moses quotes the answer to people's question about Israel's punishment of exile from the land as follows: "They went off and worshiped other gods and bowed down to them, gods they did not know, gods he had not given. Therefore, the LORD's anger burned against this land, so that he brought on it all the curses written in this book. In furious anger and in great wrath, the LORD uprooted them from their land and thrust them into another land, as it is now" (verses 26-28).

You must understand that God is amazingly patient with his people so that he sent northern Israel into exile about five hundred years after they entered the land and exiled southern Judah over one hundred years later. God's patience lasts far longer than human patience. However, his just anger must eventually happen unless real repentance takes place first. Moses' summary covers hundreds of years of God's repeated rescues and calls for the people to return to worship their invisible God instead of the false statue-gods of the nations around Israel.

Furthermore, notice the contrast of between believers and unbelievers in Psalm 119:20, 21: "My soul is consumed with longing for your laws at all times. You rebuke the arrogant, who are cursed and who stray from your commands." What young humans naturally want to obey parents' commands?

I was a passively aggressive, Pharisaical, good boy while I was growing up. I sat many hours at the supper table, after everyone else had left, refusing to eat my vegetables. When I look back on my boyhood rebellion, my refusals were understandable because those vegetables were often slimy okra and distasteful rutabagas. However, my rejection of my mother's requirements was not excusable.

Other children are outwardly-strong-willed. However, all of us rebel in one way or another against authority that we consider unjust or wrong. Thus, we're all inner or outer rebels. Therefore, according to the psalmist, we're all under God's rebuke and curse unless he rescues us with his love through faith in Jesus' perfect actions that make us eager to read, hear, and obey God's Word that tells us to obey the authorities over us.

Another Old Testament passage in the small book of Nahum describes his prophecies about Nineveh, the same city God spared from destruction in Jonah's book. In Nahum 1:2, 3a, 6a, 7, 8, the prophet's description of God alternates between his anger and his love: "The LORD is a jealous and avenging God; the LORD takes vengeance on his foes and maintains his wrath against his enemies. The LORD is slow to anger and great in power; the LORD will not leave the guilty unpunished. ... Who can withstand his indignation? Who can endure his fierce anger?... The LORD is good, a refuge in times of trouble. He cares for those who trust in him but with an overwhelming flood he will make an end of Nineveh; he will pursue his foes into darkness."

Please don't skip this passage because it disagrees with many teachers who teach that God is only a loving Father, not an angry Judge. He is both loving and just. Sadly, unbelievers around us are on their way to hell, a terribly-sad destination, unless God delivers them as he did us believers. Doesn't that fact make you thankful that he made you a believer? It should also give us a huge incentive to share God's work in our lives and what we believe about him with those unbelievers.

However, first build a loving relationship with them and seek opportunities to share your faith without trying to talk them into believing. Never argue with them. After all, God loves them as his creatures, even though he is also angry at their rebellion against him. All along the way, pray for the unbelievers around you.

<u>Bible discussion questions:</u>

1. In this section, what surprised you most? Explain.

2. How is God different from "a Santa in the sky"? Why?

3. Read Psalm 139. Which verses stand out in your mind? Why?

4. Read the author's summary of Psalm 139. What is your reaction? Explain.

5. Read Lamentations 3:55-66. What shows you that this passage is a believing lament (or complaint) to God instead of an unbelieving complaint? What is your reaction?

6. Read 2 Corinthians 5:1-10. What does Paul teach that the author says contradicts many modern ideas about what happens when we die? Explain.

7. According to the author, why are Christian beliefs not based on human fear? What do Deuteronomy 6:4, 5 and Leviticus 19:18 mean for your life practically? Why?

8. Read Psalm 119:20, 21 and Nahum chapter one. How are God's treatments of the believer and the unbeliever different? What holds us back from building relationships with the

unbelievers around us and witnessing to them about our faith? Why? How can we develop courage about sharing our faith as a replacement for our fear? Explain.

* * *

<u>One Step On Our Journey With Jesus:</u> Examine your life with persistent prayer for God's guidance to find areas of self-centeredness and wrong ideas about God and humans. Confess those areas and ideas to God persistently and ask for his assurance of pardon. Then, claiming Jesus' powerful victory, ask for his grace to improve your life.

* * *

Humor about anger along with its definition
I think that we're overdue to have a little humor about our subject. The following jokes and observations about anger come from jokebuddha.com. (I did not make up or approve of the website's address; but it, nevertheless, has some good humor and interesting sayings.)

Husband to wife: When I get mad at you, you never fight back. How do you control your anger?
Wife: I clean the toilet bowl.
Husband: How does that help?
Wife: I use your toothbrush.

Anger is a condition in which the tongue works faster than the mind.

A young girl who was writing a paper for school came to her father and asked, "Dad, what is the difference between anger and exasperation?"
The father replied, "It is mostly a matter of degree. Let me show you what I mean."
With that the father went to the telephone and dialed a number at random. To the man who answered the phone, he said, "Hello, is Melvin there?"
The man answered, "There is no one living here named Melvin. Why don't you learn to look up numbers before you dial?".
"See," said the father to his daughter. "That man was not a bit happy with our call. He was probably very busy with something and we annoyed him. Now watch...."
The father dialed the number again. "Hello, is Melvin there?" asked the father.
"Now look here!" came the heated reply. "You just called this number and I told you that there is no Melvin here! You've got lot of guts calling again!"
The receiver slammed down hard.

The father turned to his daughter and said, "You see, that was anger. Now I'll show you what exasperation means."
He dialed the same number, and when a violent voice roared, "Hello!"
The father calmly said, "Hello, this is Melvin. Have there been any calls for me?"

Depression is merely anger without the enthusiasm.

* * *

I don't recommend that anyone engage in the first and third expressions of anger at home or anywhere. However, I believe that the fourth one is an interesting way to describe a truth about the relationship between depression and anger, and the second one is a creative way to describe anger. I will investigate that idea more later in this book.

I think that we can now try to give synonyms of anger in its increasing intensity from the bottom to the top of the following list:
>
> uncontrolled rage resulting in violence,
> fury,
> outrage,
> infuriation,
> bitterness,

aggravation,
resentment,
displeasure,
frustration,
irritation.

According to dictionary.com, people generally use the word "anger" for a violent expression of displeasure.

However, I use it with the meaning "displeasure or opposition" toward something or someone, including God, arising from an unwanted circumstance in our lives or the world. It is a feeling and desire to attack or disagree with people, God, or life's circumstance that we perceive is going against us. This definition arose from some of my psychological studies.

We may not express or even be aware of that feeling and desire to criticize or oppose the objects of our anger. If we feel that our anger is unacceptable in our culture, we often bury it and store it up deep in our unconscious even from our mothers' wombs on. The problem is that we may project our unconscious anger on other people or transfer it from its past object(s) to other object(s) in the present. This observation comes directly from my experience.

In the Bible, the writers often look negatively on human anger as a selfish desire to oppose, criticize, or attack others and God. At times, though, God guides his people to attack and kill other people. Many people criticize the Bible because God tells Israel to kill every Canaanite and take over their land.

However, they fail to understand that God has told Abraham, then known as Abram, in Genesis 15:16 that "in the fourth generation, your descendants will come back here [to Canaan], for the sin of the Amorites [Canaanites] has not reached its full measure." In other words, the God of the universe as everyone's Judge has given the Canaanites four hundred years to repent of their horrendous religious practices such as killing their children during their worship of their false gods and committing sexual immorality and adultery to get their idols' favor.

Even after all the awesome miracles that God has performed when Israel has left Egypt and entered the land forty years later, the

Canaanites, who all know about God's mighty acts, have shut up their walled cities against Israel, not realizing that such actions were no obstacle against his all-powerful actions on behalf of his people.

The Judge of all the earth uses the Israelites to bring his justice on the earth after a long, patient wait and to give them the land that the Canaanites have forfeited because of their extreme religion.

Later, that same Judge ejects that generation's descendants from that same land after they have repeatedly wandered away from him and his exclusive right to their worship and service.

<u>Bible discussion questions:</u>

1. Which one of the jokes and observations about anger stands out in your mind? Why? How do they help you understand the nature of anger, both good and bad? Explain.

2. How do you respond to the author's definition of anger? Why? How do you know when you are angry? Explain.

3. What is the difference between usual human anger and righteous indignation? Instead of angrily judging people, why can't people wait until the Final Judgment to let God judge everyone justly? Explain your answers.

4. Read Matthew 7:1-5. What is wrong with condemning a whole group of people (e.g., all Muslims, Russians, or Chinese) for the actions of a minority of that group? Why?

5. How does the author defend God's requirement that Israel wipe out every Canaanite in the Promised Land? What do you think about his defense of God and the Israelites? Explain.

* * *

<u>One Step On Our Journey With Jesus</u>: Praise God for his justice in declaring lifelong, unrepentant, rebellious humans guilty as charged, but pray persistently and daily for God to work in the lives of people you know who show no evidence of loving the Lord. Resist the urge to judge them as unbelievers, since no one but God knows

their hearts and since "there but for the grace of God go I." Pray that God will enable you to let go of the urge to judge and condemn people to him as the only perfect Judge.

* * *

The Gospels' and Acts' views of human and divine anger

You've probably heard the term "righteous indignation." Well, our next passage shows it to us. Matthew 3:4-12 describes John the Baptist's message directed at the religious leaders who come to the Jordan River. John is baptizing repentant people, who respond favorably to his command from God, "Repent, for the kingdom of God is near" (verse 1). John doesn't pull any punches in saying to the leaders, "You brood of vipers! Who warned you to flee from the coming wrath? Produce fruit in keeping with repentance. And do not think you can say to yourselves, 'We have Abraham as our father'" (verse 7b-9a). John's blunt, righteous indignation is clear.

Then, he proceeds to use the future figure of Jesus the Messiah's "threshing floor" that will separate usable wheat from unusable chaff as a warning to hypocritical, unrepentant people, "He will baptize you with the Holy Spirit and with fire. His winnowing fork is in his hand, and he will clear his threshing floor, gathering his wheat into the barn and burning up the chaff with unquenchable fire" (verses 11c-12).

John expresses God's righteous indignation and criticism about the false beliefs of his day that used the Old Testament law to try to gain God's acceptance. That false religion receives the result of God's right anger forty years later, when the Romans ransack Jerusalem, burn the temple, and solidify their rule over Judea.

God gives his people those forty years to repent of their reliance on the law and their unjust murder of Jesus before he shows their descendants his righteous indignation as their just Judge.

In addition, the Final Judgment, which is still in our future, will make clear God's perfect justice toward unbelievers and his free, loving acceptance of undeserving believers only because of Jesus' victory.

Jesus' first message, according to Mark 1:15, is the same as John the Baptist's message, "The kingdom of God is near. Repent and believe the good news!" In Matthew 13:24-30, he tells an unsettling parable about a farmer who sows good seed in his field. However, at night his enemy sows weed seeds there. When all of the seeds have sprouted, his servant asks if he wants them to pull up the weeds. Instead, he tells them to wait until the harvest to discard the offending weeds.

Later, when Jesus is alone with his disciples, he explains the parable this way in Matthew 13:36-43, "The one who sowed the good seed is the Son of Man [referring to himself]. The field is the world, and the good seed stands for the sons of the kingdom. The weeds are the sons of the evil one, and the enemy who sows them is the devil. The harvest is the end of the age, and the harvesters are angels. As the weeds are pulled up and burned in the fire, so it will be at the end of the age. The Son of Man will send out his angels, and they will weed out of his kingdom everything that causes sin and all who do evil. They will throw them into the fiery furnace, where there will be weeping and gnashing of teeth. Then the righteous will shine like the sun in the kingdom of their Father. He who has ears, let him hear."

Of course, in Jesus' Sermon on the Mount (Matthew 5-7), he extends the commandment "You shall not murder" to angry words and actions (Matthew 5:21-26) and tells us not to judge and condemn other people (7:1-5). Instead, he urges us to love our enemies because God sends them his blessing of rain for their crops as well (6:43-45). To go a step further if we can't reconcile with people, forgiveness means to let go of our angry judgment about them and give our anger over to God the perfect Judge.

Our Messiah-marathon will explore soon enough how we can get the ability from God to let go of our anger. God can use all ten Holy-Spirit-refreshment stations to help us overcome any and all of our condemning attitudes.

Jesus' explanation of his parable of the wheat and the weeds unmistakably says that God's patient, righteous indignation and just anger against humans' rebellion will result in the final "harvest" of all people, a future time when people with faith in the true God of the Bible will "shine like the sun" in our perfect resurrection bodies.

On the other hand, unrepentant evil-doers will, very sadly, receive their due judgment in a place like a fiery furnace (compare its description to the lake of fire in Revelation 20), separated from God and the objects of their trust forever.

In the face of terrorism and public sins accepted by societies today, this parable should be a great comfort to believers in the 3-in-1 God of the Bible that he will judge all sin.

It should also be our incentive to spread the good news that Jesus is the only Pathway to God the Father's acceptance that gives us his gift of eternal bliss, as he claimed in John 14:6.

On the other hand, a passage that shows God's just punishment in this life is Acts 12:19b-25. Herod appears in his pompous, shiny, kingly duds in a meeting to settle a quarrel with people from up north in Tyre and Sidon. According to the Jewish historian Josephus, at the moment he appears, the early-morning sun shines brightly on his robe. Then, Luke writes, "...and the people yelled, 'This is the voice of a god, not of a man.'

Immediately, because Herod did not give praise to God, an angel of the Lord struck him down, and he was eaten by worms, and he died." Josephus' account confirms Luke's description.

God uses his angel to punish King Herod's pride with death to await the Day of Judgment.

Paul's writings and John's Revelation confirm God's justice

Not only do the Gospels and Acts testify to God's just anger and undeserved love, but Paul comforts his suffering readers with his description of the Day of Judgment in 2 Thessalonians 1:6-10: "God is just. He will pay back trouble to those who trouble you and give relief to you who are troubled and to us as well. This will happen when the Lord Jesus is revealed from heaven in blazing fire with powerful angels. He will punish those who do not know God and do not obey the gospel of our Lord Jesus. They will be punished with everlasting destruction and shut out from the presence of the Lord and the majesty of his power on the day he comes to be glorified in his holy people and to be marveled at among all those who have believed. This includes you, because you believed our testimony to you."

Several comments are needed about this passage:

(1) Paul says clearly that God is just. His words are a clear contradiction of present-day people who select only certain Scriptures and ignore others in order to limit God to his love.

(2) Our comfort when people treat us unlovingly is that God will judge them at the last day. Forgiveness means letting God judge others instead of holding on to our anger at them. It is the opposite of Adam and Eve's attempt to take over God's position by disobeying him.

(3) When others mistreat us, our hope for the Day of Judgment should increase. Are you looking forward to Jesus' Second Coming and his judgment? Are you ready for those events through faith in him?

(4) God's great fireworks will happen when Jesus returns in "blazing fire," that is, God's brightly shining glory!

(5) Unbelieving rebels will receive Jesus' justice of "everlasting destruction," which means that they will lose out on all of their power, everything, and everyone dear to them in this life, a sad but true future. However, they have brought God's judgment on themselves. They have no one to blame but themselves and will have all eternity to wail with "weeping and gnashing of teeth," in other words, great grief! It's a very sad but real truth.

(6) Notice that on that day, we who have trusted in Jesus as the only Pathway to God the Father will experience his presence with the brightness of his power, and he will be glorified (honored as a result of his brightness) in our resurrected bodies. Not only will he give true believers a public, not-guilty verdict at that day, but he will renew and perfect our bodies.

(7) He will complete our holiness as his holy people (saints) in being completely separate from the imperfections that we experience now. Oh, how I yearn for that day! Do you?

The Apostle John—an eyewitness of Jesus' life, death, resurrection, and re-entry to heaven—describes the final vision Jesus gives to him in Revelation 20-22. More specifically, in Revelation 20, he says that a thousand-year period will take place.

One main view of that millennium follows: Revelation 20:1-6 comes after 19:11-21, which figuratively depicts Jesus' Second Coming to fully vanquish his enemies. Therefore, Revelation 20:1-6 begins a new vision. This a-millennial view is that the millennium is the present age, during which God keeps Satan from preventing the good news about Jesus from spreading to all the world, after which he lets the devil loose to mobilize his troops. (I wonder if God has set Satan free since World War II and especially now with Muslim terrorism, many mass murders, and diseases. I don't know, but I suspect that is the case.)

However, we do not need to let the brutal, violent, Muslim-minority's extremism, mass murders, terrorism, and spreading viruses terrorize us, because God rules his universe, not the devil, as the first two chapters of the Book of Job clearly show. On the other hand, we need to battle Satan, not people, with God's spiritual armor, as Paul clearly says in Ephesians 6:10-20. Also, God wants to use our constant prayers (verses 18-20) as part of his victories in our personal lives and in the world.

The other main, pre-millennial view about the thousand years of Revelation 20 is that it is a literal, future 1,000 years of peace on earth when the devil's influence is minimal. However, people will still be sinful, but their sinfulness will not be public.

Take your pick between the two views, which both have their problems, but I prefer the first one, since I believe that the Book of Revelation is a series of symbolic visions similar to many other writings of that time, all depicting the time between Jesus' First and Second Comings. It seems to me that one of them concludes at the end of chapter nineteen with Jesus' Second Coming, and the final one begins with 20:1.

You may believe whatever your church believes about the millennium, because another humorous view is pan-millennialism, which says that it will all pan out! That view is very true.

In my view, Revelation 20:7-15, Jesus' vision given to John, describes in symbolic form Satan's release from restraints and his gathering of his human and angelic troops at the end of the millennium to attack God's church in verses 7-9a. "But fire came down from heaven and devoured them. And the devil, who deceived them, was thrown into the lake of burning sulfur, where the beast and the false prophet [his henchmen] had been thrown. They were tormented day and night for ever and ever" (verses 9b-10). God's right and just anger at the fallen angels' rebellion will end in their permanent exile from his presence.

At that point, whether after a future 1,000 years or the present age, John sees in his symbolic vision a great white throne and an indistinct figure (God) sitting on it. Then, the present sky and earth disappear because God replaces it with an amazing universe made new and perfect (verse 11 and Revelation 21:1).

With everyone's resurrection, God's books appear with believers' and unbelievers' names written in them. Sadly, lifelong unbelievers end up in the lake of fire (verse 15), for they have followed the devil instead of trusting in Jesus as the only Pathway to the Father.

On the other hand, believers, whose names have been written in the book of life, end up as part of the new Jerusalem (chapters 21 and 22). Finally, Death and Hades, the personified destinations of all dead people, also experience exile to the lake of fire, perhaps symbolic of God's fire that has also destroyed Sodom and Gomorrah. However, sadly, all unbelievers suffer eternally in the lake of fire with the fallen angels.

That future event of God's final, just anger should motivate us to share God's work in our lives and what we believe based on the Bible with everyone around us and to pray constantly for them. God wants to use our testimonies, prayers, and committed lives— not our control of others—to attract those he wants to rescue from their spiritual deaths to belong to him.

God's way for overcoming anxiety

Someone might ask me, "What do you think about anxiety or fear?" In my experience, my seven years of depression involved bottled-up, unconscious anger about many losses. At the deepest part of that depression, I had two severe anxiety attacks that mimicked heart attacks. (See my first book, *Doubtbusters! God Is My Shrink!*) Since God led me through this book's refreshment stations more than three decades ago, he has protected me from all anxiety attacks. I'm very thankful!

I believe that anxiety or fear often causes anger. You've probably heard about the flight or fight reaction to danger. Well, flight is fear, while fight is anger. I plan to deal with fear in a later Bible study. However, here I write that both emotions often go together in our complicated emotional lives.

On the other hand, I state without doubt that even though God feels perfect anger, he is never afraid of even Satan. The reason is that God has unlimited power, whereas the devil has only limited power and is under God's perfect, permitted rule. (See Job 1 and 2, in which God allows Satan go only so far.) His great power is available to bless and use our prayers for his kingdom to come and against

Satan's limited rule. Therefore, we don't have to fear terrorists, diseases, or any other means that the devil uses to create havoc in this fallen world.

Furthermore, he calls us to avoid fear and worry. How can we keep from being afraid? I found that God used the refreshment-station, ten-step process to overcome my stored-up fears as well as my anger.

<u>Bible discussion questions:</u>

1. Read Matthew 3:4-12. What is your reaction to John the Baptist's righteous indignation? Why do you feel that way?

2. Read Matthew 13:24-30, 36-43. How do you feel about Jesus' parable and his explanation? What is your response to the author's comments? Why do you feel that way?

3. Read Matthew 5:21-26. How do you respond to Jesus' extension of murder to selfish anger? Why?

4. Read 2 Thessalonians 1:6-10. What do you think people who deny that God is the just Judge expressing his wrath and anger at human rebellion do with this passage? Which of the author's seven comments stand out in your mind, either positively or negatively? Why?

5. Read Revelation 19:11 through chapter 20. Which interpretation of the thousand-year period (a-millennial, pre-millennial, and/or pan-millennial) appeals to you? Why? What do you think about the author's explanation of his view of Revelation 20? Explain.

6. How you feel about the author's comments about anxiety or fear? Why?

* * *

<u>One Step On Our Journey With Jesus:</u> Praise God in many prayers for his perfect justice and love. Pray that through Jesus' victory, God will change your self-centered anger and anxiety to God-centered love and trust, escape from fear, and righteous indignation at sins, not sinners. Be sure to follow the rest of the spiritual refreshment stations in this book by putting them into

practice with the goal of receiving God's promised peace.

* * *

Our Father's tough-love discipline of his children

God's tough-love in the Old Testament
I've spent a lot of space establishing the biblical fact that God shows just anger as our rightful Judge because so many people these days deny that God has that quality. Now, I turn to a biblical theme that is not very personally pleasant but is necessary to round out our view of God and move on to other refreshment stations in running our spiritual marathon toward the finish-line, where God's lasting peace awaits us.

How does our heavenly Father discipline us believers? Psalm 119, which celebrates God's revealed will in his Word, has some inspired observations on that topic. For example, verses 20 and 21 set up a contrast between the believing writer and unbelievers, "My soul is consumed with longing for your laws at all times. You rebuke the arrogant, who are cursed and stray from your commands." In this case, God's rebuke is reserved for those who have self-centered pride, but the psalmist points up the need for us believers to hunger and thirst for Bible truths. How hungry are we for the Bible's history and teachings?

In addition, the psalmist writes about the good that God brought out of his discipline of the writer in verses 67, 68, and 71: "Before I was afflicted, I went astray, but now I obey your word. You are good, and what you do is good; teach me your decrees.... It was good for me to be afflicted so that I might learn your decrees." The writer says that in his experience, God has used his struggles to point him back to obeying God's Word. How has God made you more willing, because of the suffering and losses of your life, to follow his will, eager to pray, and want to listen to preachers and teachers who share his Word?

Another passage about God's discipline as our heavenly Father is Proverbs 3:11, 12: "My son, do not despise the LORD's discipline and do not resent his rebuke, because the LORD disciplines those he loves, as a father the son he delights in." All parents can relate to these verses, because we must set limits for our children and discipline them when they go beyond our requirements to teach them obedience. God makes parents his agents of loving discipline of our children. How else are children going to learn respect for human and divine authority in their lives?

Furthermore, notice in this part of God's Word that the LORD (Yahweh) disciplines us as his sons and daughters. That name for God describes his eternal faithfulness to his personal relationship (covenant) with his adopted children. The fact that he is like a parent who is always loving in his discipline for our good is enormously comforting to us. It gives us security within his limits described in the Bible. Of course, when we step outside of his limits, he allows and causes his tough-love discipline.

On the other hand, we must not have the false idea that when people experience great suffering, they have sinned in some great way. Job and his "friends" have that false assumption. Job complains to God because he has led a blameless (not perfect) life that is genuinely committed to God, the blamelessness with which writer describes him at the book's beginning. He asks why, therefore, has he experienced such severe suffering? However, his "friends" judge him as a great sinner because of his suffering.

Job, his wife, and his "friends" don't realize that Job's extreme struggles are a test of his faith's endurance and a blessing for his spiritual improvement. Yes, God lovingly allows all losses and trials in our lives in order to teach us lessons about him and his relationship with us. They are all God's ways to give us spiritual improvement and progress. For example, we may need to be humbled from our pride that tempts us to do our activities without relying on God.

Notice also in the verses in Proverbs, that God's love for and delight in us motivates him to discipline us through our reading, study, and listening to his Word, the Bible. When we stop reading, studying, and obeying his Word, he gently but firmly allows hardships in our lives that point us back to his revealed will. We never arrive at perfection in this life but always need God's direction through the Bible.

God's tough love in the New Testament
Now, we are ready for Hebrews 12:1-13, a passage commenting on Proverbs 3:11, 12. In

Hebrews 11, the writer has listed many of the Old Testament people of faith whose lives show trust in God even though they don't see him but hold on to their faith with a firm hope of their bright future after their death. Then, he writes in Hebrews 12:1 his application of chapter 11 to his readers' lives, "Therefore, since we are surrounded by such a great cloud of witnesses [the Old Testament saints], let us throw off everything that hinders and the sin that so easily entangles and let us run with perseverance the race marked out for us."

Perhaps you thought that I came up with the idea of a marathon all on my own, but this one and other New Testament passages also compare our Christian lives to running a race. I confess, I believe that God wanted me to borrow the idea, but he also led me to the comparison of our God's blessings in our lives with his refreshment stations along the way.

After all, God receives all of the credit for all little and big activities that we're good at. If you doubt my statement, read Isaiah 28:23-29, especially verses 26 and 29, where God tells Israel that he teaches the farmer how to farm. By application, all the actions that you and I accomplish are really God's blessings coming to us through the experiences, education, and training that he has given us.

Thus, the Bible teaches that God is intimately involved in all of life to bless his created beings. As a result, it overcomes the secularism in many cultures that separates our experiences from God and the self-centered pragmatism that depends on human experiences to go through life.

As we get back to Hebrews 12:2, we notice that the writer shares with us the Starting-Line, Pathway, Refreshment Stations, and Finish-Line of our marathon. They are all summarized in Jesus: "Let us fix our eyes on Jesus, the author and perfecter of our faith, who for the joy set before him endured the cross, scorning its shame, and sat down at the right hand of the throne of God." Don't just read these words of Scripture, but let them sink into your heart, which biblically involves your thinking, feeling, and deciding.

First, we notice that Jesus joyfully and actively decides to submit to Roman injustice and torture! How can he experience joy in the middle of such a horrible, embarrassing death? Notice that his joy is set before him; that is, it is future joy. Why? He focuses on you and me as believers coming to miraculous faith and, more immediately, on his resurrection and return to the Father's place of authority in heaven.

Second, Jesus begins our faith as its Author and will perfect it when we die. That fact gives him all of the honor for our faith-marathon and takes away any credit we might be tempted to claim for ourselves as lifelong marathoners.

Third, God prompts the writer's command to keep our spiritual eyes trained on Jesus as we run our long-distance race because we often take our eyes off him to worry and get angry about our trying circumstances, which God allows to mold us more and more into his likeness.

After the writer to the Hebrews quotes Proverbs 3:11, 12, God guides him to write, "Endure hardship as discipline; God is treating you as sons [his adopted children]....If you are not disciplined (and everyone undergoes discipline), then you are

illegitimate children and not true sons"
(verses 7a, 8).

Here is God's warning about our lives. He
uses the writer to test our lives to discover
whether we are true believers. We need to be
growing to be more like Jesus as a result of
God's Word and prayer in reaction to the
trials that God allows. If we aren't changing
with greater commitment and eagerness to
follow God's will, we need to pray for the
Holy Spirit's renewal through Jesus' powerful
victory.

The writer goes on to compare God's
discipline with that of our parents, "Our
fathers disciplined us for a little while as they
thought best; but God disciplines us for our
good, that we may share in his holiness. No
discipline seems pleasant at the time but
painful. Later on, then, it produces a harvest
of righteousness and peace for those who
have been trained by it" (Hebrews 12:10, 11).
Several thoughts come to mind about these
two verses:

(1) He talks about our parents' discipline. My
parents were opposites as far as their
discipline was concerned and in just about

every other way. Mom was an overly-strict, legalistic Christian; whereas Dad was an overly-permissive, pragmatic unbeliever. Since they never agreed on how to discipline us three boys, I was a mixed-up, middle kid.

(2) Of course, all of us grew up with imperfect parents with some degree of dysfunction in our families because of favoritism and inconsistent discipline. Sadly, some of us experienced physical, emotional, and/or sexual abuse. If you will run this whole marathon, you can find God's gift of inner peace about your childhood "junk," if you seek and find God's power to persevere in running the race.

(3) In contrast, God as our perfect Parent knows how to discipline us perfectly. We often can't see the good results that he will bring out of some struggle that he has allowed. However, since he has promised to cause good results in our lives, we know that he will fulfill his promises.

(4) Notice that God means to grow a "harvest of righteousness and peace" through his discipline. If we are true believers, God has already transferred Jesus' righteousness to us

to give us our permanent, not-guilty standing before God the Judge. In other words, we are already fully right with God, our Judge, because of Jesus' life and death.

(5) The crop of righteousness that the writer mentions here as a result of God's discipline is the right living that God will add to our right standing and that he will make grow throughout our lifetimes by way of Jesus' victory and the Holy Spirit's work.

(6) The other part of God's harvest crop is peace. Here again, Jesus has accomplished our outer peace with God our Judge once and for all. He has made us his friends and followers instead of the enemies we were when God caused our conceptions in our mothers' wombs.

(7) However, God also wants to give us his peace in our hearts about our losses and struggles. That emotional peace is the subject of this book, and Jesus is our only Pathway to that inner peace, as he himself said, "I am the way and the truth and the life; no one comes to the Father except through me" (John 14:6).

One final Bible passage at our first refreshment station is 1 Peter 4:12-19. In those verses, Peter tells his suffering readers not to be surprised at their trials, but to "rejoice that you participate in the sufferings of Christ, so that you may be overjoyed when his glory is revealed. If you are insulted because of the name of Christ, you are blessed, for the Spirit of glory and of God rests on you.... If you suffer as a Christian, do not be ashamed, but praise God that you bear that name. For it is time for judgment to begin with the family of God; and if it begins with us, what will the outcome be for those who do not obey the gospel of God?... So then, those who suffer according to God's will should commit themselves to their faithful Creator and continue to do good" (verses 13, 14, 16, 17, 19). Notice some of Peter's inspired teachings:

(1) We are to rejoice that we are part of Jesus' sufferings when he allows us to go through trials. The writer to the Hebrews and Peter agree on the teaching that because Jesus has experienced the joy about the final results in our lives, we should also joyfully go through this life's sorrows. I can tell you from personal experience that joy and grief can go together. We'll see more of this seemingly impossible combination as we run our marathon.

(2) However, how are our trials and losses part of Jesus' suffering, since he suffered only once on the cross, not many times? Of course, Peter cannot mean that somehow when we suffer, God justifies us by making us not guilty. No, his verdict of not guilty and our standing that we are right with God because of Jesus' death happens only once at the time we first believe.

(3) Peter definitely means God's daily cleansing of our rebellion that still exists in our sinful nature resulting in our anger and anxiety. He wants us to progress toward our marathon journey. Therefore, he disciplines us for our good. It's his tough love shown to us by our heavenly Father.

(4) Some Christians experience persecution from intolerant people. Should they lash out at them to argue and defend God? Peter says that we should not be ashamed but, instead, we must praise God that we can stand in his strength as a witness for him.

(5) Then, Peter says that the reason for our need of endurance in the face of opposition is that "it is time for judgment to begin with the family of God." Peter uses here the word

"judgment" with the meaning of "discipline"
in contrast to God's punishment of
unbelievers at the last day.

(6) God's challenge through Peter is that we
need to pray for the power of Jesus' victory to
be able to give our lives more and more to
"our faithful Creator and continue to do
good."

* * *

The following humorous and serious quotes
are from goodreads.com:

"I hate paying my income tax."
"You should be a good citizen. Why don't you pay
with a smile?"
"I'd like to, but they insist on money!"

Speak when you are angry, and you will make the
best speech you will ever regret."—Ambrose Brice

"Letting go gives us freedom, and freedom is the only
condition for happiness. If, in our heart, we still cling
to anything - anger, anxiety, or possessions - we
cannot be free."—Thích Nhất Hạnh, *The Heart of the
Buddha's Teaching: Transforming Suffering into
Peace, Joy, and Liberation*

"Anger is an acid that can do more harm to the vessel in which it is stored than to anything on which it is poured."—Mark Twain

The Buddhist quote is true; but Buddhism never asks *why* they should do good. It is a human-centered, not God-centered, approach to life. Instead, it's Jesus who sets us free from our self-centered approach to our emotions and possessions.

The second and fourth sayings are good commentaries on the emotion of anger, while the first one is just for our enjoyment.

What's the point of our marathon's first refreshment station?

Someone might ask me why we need to understand God's just anger at the beginning of our spiritual marathon. My reason for my use of these Bible passages during the first leg and at the first two refreshment stations of our marathon is that until we understand that God is the just Judge and that Jesus has satisfied our divine Judge's right anger and his guilty verdict against us because of his great love for us, we cannot run our race with great, constant joy in order to receive his gift of inner peace in this life at the finish-line.

Furthermore, we have also seen that God's Word clearly balances his anger and love. In fact, we will see that he shows his discipline of us solely because he loves us enough to improve our lives to be more like Jesus.

<u>Bible discussion questions:</u>

(1) How do you respond to the biblical idea that God shows "tough love" to his people? Explain. How has he shown that love to you?

(2) Read Psalm 119:20, 21, 67, 68, 71 and Proverbs 3:11, 12. How is God's punishment of unbelievers (Psalm 119:21) different from his discipline of believers? Whose fault is it that the arrogant stray from God's ways, and whose responsibility is it that they will, sadly, end up in hell? Why do you feel that way?

(3) Why do you suppose that the author describes God's treatment of believers in the Bible as tough love? How much do you agree with him? What experiences of his tough love have people you know had? What were the good results? Explain.

(4) Read Job 1 and 2. Of what heavenly drama was Job ignorant when he suffered severe losses? How do these chapters show the relationships among God, Satan, and us in our trials and suffering? What comfort do you find from this passage for times when you also will suffer? Explain.

(5) Read Hebrews 12:1-13 and 1 Peter 4:12-19. Summarize both writers' teachings about believers' suffering. What is the relationship between Jesus' suffering and ours? What comfort do you gain from these passages? Explain.

(6) Re-read the author's last two paragraphs. Summarize his thoughts. In the light of all of the Bible verses we have studied during this part of our marathon, how much do you agree with his conclusion? Why?

* * *

One Step On Our Journey With Jesus: If you are going through trials in your life, first praise God, your Potter, that he is molding you as his clay to be more like Jesus. Pray that God will show you his lessons that he wants you to learn. Always

pray for God's gift of spiritual progress based on Jesus' death and resurrection.

Life's Emotional Marathon Part II: Understand human emotions.

Now that we understand a little more about God's perfect emotions, our marathon's course involves our running through the muddy waters of human emotions by, first of all, stopping at:

Refreshment Station 3: Understand your conscious, subconscious, and unconscious minds.

My first assumption during this refreshment station is the Bible's clear teaching that God created all humans. In Genesis 1:26, 27, inspired Moses declares, "Then [after God made the animals], he "said, 'Let us make man in our image, in our likeness, and let them rule over the fish of the sea and the birds of the air, over the livestock, over all the earth, and over all the creatures that move along the ground. So, God created man in his own image. In the image of God, he created him, male and female, he created them."

Second, since God made us like him in some ways, we also have the emotion of anger. However, we have seen that after Adam and Eve and all of us humans have descended into rebellion, Cain shows how self-centered his anger becomes after the Eden fiasco by killing his brother Abel (Genesis 4:2b-16).

Amazingly, God shows his love and grace by protecting Cain from being killed in spite of his sinful murder. However, he goes on to be the father of the unrepentant, unbelieving line from Adam and Eve.

On the other hand, Adam and Eve's son Seth was the head of the believing ancestry line until Cain's line intermarries with Seth's descendants. Genesis 6:1 describes that sad fact.

Then, God gives the human race one hundred and twenty years to return to him (Genesis 6:2), while Noah builds the ark, which protects his family from the disaster of the worldwide flood and is a warning to humans that God's patience doesn't last forever but endures a lot longer than human patience.

My third assumption is that God makes our emotional life very complex with several levels. That idea is a fact, since God reveals himself as the Creator and Guide of the universe through two eyeglasses, the creation itself and the Bible (see Psalm 19). Furthermore, the Bible is the set of eyeglasses through which we need to understand the fallen universe.

For example, the Bible assumes that God has made and continues to guide all of his non-human creation (Genesis 1:1-25). Then, he has created the first human, Adam, out of the dust of the earth to be like him in some ways as his special creation (Genesis 1:26—2:7). Then, he makes Eve out of Adam. If God reveals truth through his creation, he uses the discoveries of scientific fact, not every theory, to reveal information about his creation.

As a result, we can learn God's truth about the human personality from the sciences, as long as those findings aren't in conflict with the Bible's truths.

However, in the area of psychological information, a great deal of controversy has arisen about whether our mind has more than a conscious part. The problem is that many psychological experts are behavioral scientists who only accept what can be measured scientifically. As a result, they question the theory of Sigmund Freud that our minds have conscious, subconscious, and unconscious parts.

First of all, in approaching this subject, we go to Jeremiah's description of two kinds of humans, believers and unbelievers, in chapter seventeen. He observes in verse nine after both of those portraits, "The heart is deceitful above all things and beyond cure. Who can understand it?" Well, I believe that God has used Sigmund Freud, even though he probably wasn't aware of God's guidance, to provide us with insights into our minds.

Second, how can I side with Freud over many modern scientific counselors who deny that our minds have unconscious and subconscious aspects? Well, as Jeremiah says, our human hearts, the centers of our personalities, are hard to understand and certainly beyond human cure apart from God's blessings.

Moreover, in my experience, I was completely unaware of my buried, unconscious anger for the first forty-three years of my life, but God broke through to me to reveal my growing bitterness that had resulted in seven years of major depression and two anxiety attacks at the depth of my depression. He used a therapy group, psychological professionals, and group activities to make me aware of my deep-seated anger that had been in my unconscious mind for all of my life since my conception, literally.

I won't detail here how God gave me such self-discoveries, because I shared those amazing, powerful events in my books *Doubtbusters! God Is My Shrink!* and *Be Bolder Growin' Older* (both available from Amazon). I recommend them for your reading pleasure and benefit. My autobiography, *What God Has Done: Peace Like a River*, will be published in the near future.

However, I didn't share the following experience with the readers of my other books. After God used psychological professionals to make my anger emerge from my unconscious, a couple of them led our group into a room that had an old table and stacks of newspapers. The idea was that we had to make newspaper-clubs with tape. Then, they invited us to imagine what that table symbolized in our minds and pummel it with all of our might as long as it would take to express our feelings.

Well, I taped together a huge newspaper-club so that it took all of my strength to pound that rickety table. I imagined that it stood for my forty-three years of repressed (unknown) anger. I then attacked it with a ferocity that I didn't know I possessed for many minutes until I sweat buckets (or so it seemed). However, that plucky table survived six people's severe pounding.

What did I learn from all of those experiences? First, I discovered that my mind had more than what I was conscious of. Second, the table experience made my accumulated anger surface from my unconscious. Third, that exhausting time taught me that I wasn't going to decrease my anger by pounding a table; expressing my anger during only one session was not going to help me overcome my anger and depression.

Well, what overcame my anger and anxiety and will overcome your anger? That, dear reader, is the subject of our marathon. Therefore, my suggestion is that you persevere through some difficult "running."

Another relevant Bible passage is Zechariah 12:1-5, where the prophet quotes God as saying in verses 1-3 and 5, "This is the word of the LORD concerning Israel. The LORD, who stretches out the heavens, who lays the foundation of the earth, and who forms the spirit of man [humanity] within him, declares: 'I am going to make Jerusalem a cup that sends all the surrounding peoples reeling. Judah will be besieged as well as Jerusalem. On that day, when all the nations of the earth are gathered against her, I will make Jerusalem an immovable rock for all the nations. All who try to move it will injure themselves.' Then [after God's defeat of the nations], the leaders of Judah will say in their hearts, 'The people of Jerusalem are strong, because the LORD Almighty is their God.'"

A number of observations come to mind about these verses:

(1) This passage demonstrates the truth many Bible passages teach that these verses are from God alone. We know that such an

amazing claim is true because its content is beyond human thought. God, therefore, has definitely inspired the Bible.

(2) Notice that God claims that he has made the heavens, that is, the universe beyond the earth; the world; and the human spirit or life, with which he makes contact when he gives us faith to believe in and follow him.

(3) God mentions that the human spirit is his creation on a par with the earth and the rest of the universe. You can be sure that your life is very important to God, since he has created it. In addition, he has created your unconscious mind, but we have often filled it with junk-feelings about past events. We must uncover those feelings about events in our lives and find his strength to release them to God in order to receive his peace. Often, that kind of discovery requires someone else's help.

(4) The picture of the unbelieving nations surrounding and attacking Jerusalem is similar to Satan's gathering of all unbelievers in Revelation 20:9a, "They marched across the breadth of the earth and surrounded the camp of God's people, the city he loves." I would assume that a number of people would

jump to the conclusion that the verse refers to present-day Jerusalem in present-day Israel. However, the city is what would become the new Jerusalem, which has twelve gates with the names of the twelve tribes of Israel (Revelation 21:12) and twelve foundations with the names of Jesus' apostles (Revelation 21:14).

(5) Therefore, I draw the conclusion that the city of Jerusalem in Zechariah 12:1-5 is a symbolic picture of all Old and New Testament believers, since the New Testament definitely points in that direction. The international church, God's new Jerusalem, calls all Jews and everyone else to follow Jesus, the only divine-human Pathway to the Father's acceptance and to his gift of full inner and outer peace.

(6) According to this passage and Revelation 20 and 21, God will defeat the unbelieving nations. Jesus says as much in Revelation 20:9b to the Apostle John, "But fire came down from heaven and devoured them." Of course, this verse has a similar meaning to God's destruction of openly-rebellious and homosexually-immoral Sodom and Gomorrah, when "the LORD rained down

burning sulfur on Sodom and Gomorrah—
from the LORD out of the heavens" (Genesis
19:24).

(7) The people of Jerusalem (all Old and New
Testament believers) in the Zechariah passage
will give full credit in praise to God for his
victory over evil. Such a thought is a
recurring biblical theme that God defeats
strong evil with his power using human
weakness.

(8) If we follow his leading through his Word
during our marathon journey, he will give us
his inner peace as a foretaste of the final,
perfect peace in his new universe (Revelation
21).

Examining three parts of our human personalities

Now, we need to do a short examination of
Freud's idea that rings true. On the one hand,
I don't agree with his claim that all human
motivation is comes from the sexual drive. On
the other hand, I do believe that God has used
him to reveal truth about the human
personality. He believed on the basis of his
patients' experiences and his counseling of

them that the conscious self is only the tip of the personality iceberg, about 10% of the self.

The next part of the personality is the subconscious. It is about 20% to 30% of the personality and consists of our reactions to recent events that we have suppressed and that we can easily recall. When we suppress some feeling or thought, we are aware of it, whereas when we repress it, we are no longer aware of it.

I repressed my anger and anxiety so much that large parts of my emotional reactions to my many losses disappeared completely from my conscious and subconscious minds only to reappear in my physical body.

The remaining part of the human spirit is the unconscious, in which we repress many emotions without knowing it. A personal example is my loss of my three-year-old brother to leukemia when I was two and a half months old. I know that my family's great stress over Bobby's sickness affected me even in my mother's womb, since scientists have found that a high level of family stress does affect an unborn baby.

Another example is our second son's death from that same disease. I wept a few tears at his bedside but went back to work as a teacher after his funeral, thinking that I had finished grieving Keith's death. The trouble was that I repressed my anger and anxiety about both deaths in my unconscious mind. My emotions about those events and others in my life developed into seven years of major depression beginning seven years after Keith's death.

My point is that God wants to uncover our repressed feelings hiding in our unconscious mind in order to give us his lasting peace about those events that triggered our hidden anger and anxiety that surface at times. May God use the rest of our emotional marathon to give us his lasting peace, not the world's temporary, variable peace, at our finish-line.

However, the question may arise why I use Freud's insights into human psychology. After all, he wasn't a Christian. My answer is that God has revealed himself in his creation. David wrote in Psalm 19:1, "The heavens declare the glory of God, the skies proclaim the work of his hands."

Also, Paul wrote, "The wrath of God is being revealed from heaven against all the godlessness and wickedness of men who suppress the truth by their wickedness, since what may be known about God is plain to them because God has made it plain to them. For since the creation of the world God's invisible qualities—his eternal power and divine nature—have been clearly seen, being understood from what has been made, so that men are without excuse" (Romans 1:18-20).

David and Paul agree that God reveals the truth about himself in his creation, including Freud. Humanity's primary sin is to reject God's revealing of himself through his handiwork. Thus, God has used psychiatrists since Freud to help many people overcome their anger and anxiety, whether or not they are aware of God's assistance. Dear reader, God used a variety of such great people to rid me of my major, seven-year depression for more than three decades, and I praise him for his rescue.

If you doubt my point, the Bible presents the same teaching. God used unbelieving Assyria to eject thoroughly rebellious northern Israel from the Promised Land. He also used pagan King Cyrus to return his people there.

Now, the time is overdue for some more quotes about anger from goodreads.com:

"Learn this from me. Holding anger is a poison. It eats you from inside. We think that hating is a weapon that attacks the person who harmed us. But hatred is a curved blade. And the harm we do, we do to ourselves."—Mitch Albom, *The Five People You Meet in Heaven*

"Don't hold onto anger, hurt, or pain. They steal your energy and keep you from love."—Leo Buscaglia

If you try to get rid of fear and anger without knowing their meaning, they will grow stronger and return."—Deepak Chopra, *The Third Jesus: The Christ We Cannot Ignore*

"Swearing doesn't make your argument valid; it just tells the other person you have lost your class and control." —Shannon L. Alder.

My previous observation holds true that we can learn God's truth from these writers. I never know for sure whether a writer or anyone else is a Christian or not, because only God knows their hearts. However, I can only measure their ideas in the light of God's inspired Word.

As I wrote the previous paragraph about people's hearts, Matthew 15:17-20 came to mind to illustrate my point about Freud's insights into our conscious, subconscious, and unconscious minds. Jesus illustrates his defense of his followers' failure to follow the Pharisees' petty rules about ceremonial cleansing before meals by saying to his disciples, "Don't you see that whatever enters the mouth goes into the stomach and then out of the body? But the things that come out of the mouth come from the heart, and these make a man "unclean.' For out of the heart come evil thoughts, murder, adultery, sexual immorality, theft, false testimony, slander. These are what make a man 'unclean'; but eating with unwashed hands does not make him 'unclean.'"

In the Bible, the word "heart" almost never refers the pumping, physical organ. Instead, it figuratively means the center of our personality's feeling, thinking, and deciding. Jesus points out that we have a lot of stored-up evil in our hearts.

For example, a person may learn that someone is living with a person of the opposite sex without marrying that person first, a clear sin called sexual immorality or fornication in the Bible. What should the first person do with that information? If that person has stored up a lot of anger about the past, the temptation is to spread that juicy tidbit to other acquaintances to judge the people's sins.

In the case of my anger, I had no desire to spread gossip about people, but I yelled without swearing at other drivers for cutting me off or going too slowly. My intense anger sometimes came out at people from my unconscious mind because of their comparatively unimportant ideas or actions.

At any rate, Jesus in Matthew 18:15-17 tells us, "If your brother sins against you, go and show him his fault, just between the two of you. If he listens to you, you have won your brother over. But if he will not listen, take one or two others along.... If he refuses to listen to them, tell it to church...." My point is that Jesus teaches us to confront the believing sinner (our "brother") lovingly with his sinful conduct instead of angrily talking behind his back to make us feel better about ourselves or with other self-centered motives.

You see, our actions sometimes reveal our unconscious anger without our realizing it.

<u>**Bible Discussion Questions:**</u>

1. Summarize the author's interweaving of Bible passages, his personal experiences, and Sigmund Freud's idea about the human personality at the beginning of this refreshment station. What point is the author making? How much do you agree or disagree with the author? Why?

2. Read Zechariah 12:1-5. What point does the author make about God's creation of the human spirit? Which one of the author's comments on that passage stands out in your mind? Why?

3. What are the three parts of the human personality, according to Sigmund Freud? What value do you see in understanding his theory? Explain.

4. How relevant are the author's experiences of his brother's and son's deaths? Why does he share his trauma? How did his unconscious anger surface? In general, how do Christians' anger show up nowadays? What can we do about it when they use us as the objects of their anger? Explain.

5. Read Psalm 19:1 and Romans 1:18-20. What teaching do David and Paul give to us? How does the author relate that teaching to his use of Freud's personality theory? How much do you agree with him? Explain.

6. Read Matthew 15:17-20 and the author's comments. How relevant is that discussion in connection with the author's comments about gossip as an example of people's unconscious anger showing up? Why do you feel that way?

* * *

One Step On Our Journey With Jesus: Ask God to help you recall how you have shown the anger in your life to others. Then, confess to him ways you have hurt others with your anger. Share your anger and anxiety about the past with God in prayer as you continue "running" this book's marathon. If you can't identify those emotions in your life, seek someone's help to uncover them.

* * *

Furthermore, Paul begins his wonderful chapter five of the Book of Romans by declaring that "there is no condemnation for those who are in Christ Jesus" because of Jesus' finished work on the Roman torture tree (verses 1-4). In other words, God-man Jesus ran a perfect marathon that we could never run so that he strengthens us to run toward his promised gift of inner peace.

Paul then wrote about two opposing kinds of human mind in Romans 5:5-8: "Those who live according to the sinful nature have their minds set on what that nature desires, but those who live in accordance with the Spirit have their minds set on what the Spirit desires. The mind of sinful man is death, but the mind controlled by Spirit is life and peace; the sinful mind is hostile to God. It does not submit to God's law, nor can it do so. Those controlled by the sinful nature cannot please God." We can glean many instructive thoughts from this passage:

(1) Notice that if God has connected us permanently with Jesus through his grace ("in Christ Jesus"), our just Judge no longer "condemns" us. Rather than the guilty standing which we inherited when God enabled us to be conceived, Jesus' death gives us the legal standing of not-guilty, which

means that we are free of God's condemnation!

(2) When God our Father has sent Jesus to his death, he looks forward to ushering us into the very presence of the whole universe's Ruler. The result is that we can and should pray to him all the time. He will not condemn or even snicker at our prayers but, instead, will answer them "yes," "no," "not yet," or "not the way you expect."

(3) We, then, become God's advisors. What can keep us from praying to him all the time, since he accepts us as his friends and always hears our communications?

(4) If we have even a small amount of faith in Jesus as the only Pathway into our Father's powerful presence, we are united to God similar to a tree branch to its trunk or, as Jesus explains in John 15, a grape branch to its vine. In that way, like the branch, we depend on Jesus for our life and strength to live for God, not for ourselves.

(5) Remember that it only takes a little amount of faith to be connected to Jesus and

have the Spirit-led mind Paul describes. Of course, he wants our faith to grow.

(6) He then writes about two minds in different people. One mind focuses on seeking satisfaction and security from earthly people and things, while the other one is Spirit-led. When we come to believe in and desire to follow Jesus as our Pathway and Guide to our Father in heaven, God supernaturally gives us our new minds that think, desire, and feel what the Holy Spirit thinks, desires, and feels. However, our new, Spirit-led minds assert themselves over our old minds throughout our whole lives, as Paul describes in Romans 6:1-14 and 7:8-25.

(7) God uses his gifts of tough-love experiences to replace our selfish minds with our Spirit-led minds, including our feelings.

In all of Paul's inspired letters, he contrasts two natures at work in us, the old sinful nature and the God-given, new nature. For example, the church at Corinth in present-day southern Greece was one of his problem churches. They were at the intersection of two trade routes on that peninsula and were in danger of relapsing from the true faith. He wrote them in 2 Corinthians 11:2-3, "I am jealous for you with a godly jealousy. I promised you to one husband, to Christ, so that I might present you as a pure virgin to him. But I am afraid that just as Eve was deceived by the serpent's cunning, your minds may somehow be led astray from your sincere and pure devotion to Christ."

Either the main commitment of people's lives, pictured by marriage, is to Jesus or to the devil. We are conceived in our mothers' wombs married to Satan; and when God gives us his miraculous new birth (John 3:1-18), the battle between him and the devil begins and continues throughout our lives. Beyond the basic, conscious set of decisions that his new birth causes in our lives, our minds always have an unconscious set of emotions that are in conflict—God's joy and peace as his gifts *versus* selfish emotions such as anger and anxiety caused by difficult past events that rob us of his joy and peace at times.

Moreover, in Ephesians 4:20-24, after Paul describes the Ephesians' previous selfish life dedicated to the devil, he writes, "You, however, did not come know Christ that way. Surely you heard of him and were taught in him in accordance with the truth that is in Jesus. You were taught, with regard to your former way of life to put off your old self, which is being corrupted with its deceitful desires; to be made new in the attitude of you minds; and to put on the new self, created to be like God in true righteousness and holiness." Paul's picture here is our responsibility to take off the old, dirty, self-centered "clothes" of our inborn nature and to replace them with the new self having God's right and holy "clothes."

In Ephesians 1-3, Paul has described God's choice of us from before his creation of the universe, his unearned rescue of us by grace through faith, the church's unity in Jesus' love, and God as the Source of the power for our new life. Then, in chapters 4-6, he calls us to take up our responsibility to reject more and more our old nature and to grow in his new nature.

That effort is the reason we are running our marathon, because of God's call through Jesus in the Holy Spirit's strength. After all, our part is totally to the 3-in-1 God's credit because all of our new strength to run toward the goal of emotional peace comes from him.

Therefore, the Apostle Paul gives his blessing or prayer to the Thessalonians and to us in his first letter as God's encouragement during our marathon as follows: "May God himself, the God of peace, sanctify you through and through. May your whole spirit, soul, and body be kept blameless at the coming of our Lord Jesus Christ. The one who calls you is faithful and he will do it" (5:23, 24).

Notice some very helpful ideas here in this part of God's Word:
(1) God is the God of peace. That is, Jesus as the Pathway to God provides us who believe in him outer peace with our Father-Judge. The moment we receive Jesus' death as our gateway to God's free acceptance (grace), we change from God's enemies to his friends.

(2) Also, God has promised to give us inner peace from the tornado that our anger and anxiety can cause in our conscious and unconscious minds.

(3) That lasting peace is the result of our following the Bible's pattern of prayer outlined there.

(4) In this way, God does the ongoing process of "sanctifying" us, that is, making us more and more holy or separate from the sinful imperfections in our "whole spirit, soul, and body." However, if we are unaware of the self-centered anger and anxiety in our unconscious, how will God "sanctify" us fully?

(5) As we have seen, he calls us to our responsibility to cooperate with him in uncovering those imperfections, no matter how painful those discoveries may be. They are often very difficult to face.

(6) Paul prays that we may be blameless at Jesus' return. According to the Old Testament background, blamelessness means a genuinely committed, outward life of faith before God, not perfection. The Old Testament word refers to the animals slaughtered and offered in substitution for the Israelites; they have had to be without all outward defects. God's Word describes Noah and Job as blameless, but they are far from perfect. Noah gets drunk one night after the flood, while Job questions God's part in his great losses and repents after God confronts him with his pride.

(7) God's great comfort for us weak, fallen believers is Paul's blessing that he who has called us "is faithful and he will do it." As we run on his marathon-Pathway to inner peace, he will give us his power to persevere in making our difficult run, resulting in his gift of inner peace.

The following are some interesting and helpful sayings about anger:

"And I just want to tell you, at some point it doesn't matter who was right and who was wrong. At some point, being angry is just another bad habit, like smoking, and you keep poisoning yourself without thinking about it."—Jonathan Tropper, *This is Where I Leave You*

"Sometimes I think there's a beast that lives inside me, in the cavern that's where my heart should be, and every now and then it fills every last inch of my skin, so that I can't help but do something inappropriate. Its breath is full of lies; it smells of spite."—Jodi Picoult, *Handle with Care*

"Get mad, then get over it. "—Colin Powell

"Let today be the day you finally release yourself from the imprisonment of past grudges and anger. Simplify your life. Let go of the poisonous past and live the abundantly beautiful present... today."

— Steve Maraboli, *Unapologetically You: Reflections on Life and the Human Experience*

"Quiet anger frightens me. The drunks, the idiots, the ones that rage easily - them I can handle. I know when to step out of their way. It's the ones that hold the anger in, the men that think about what they do and how they do it, that scare me. They're the ones that cause damage."—Katie McGarry, *Dare You To*

I found the first quote interesting for our long run since he says that anger poisons us without our thinking about it (the unconscious). The next one comparing anger to an inner beast is an interesting analogy. Colin Powell's advice is good but hard to follow, since anger keeps receding into our unconscious. The fourth advice is also very difficult to perform for the same reason. Finally, the fifth observation is very true because quiet men in their 20s who keep to themselves commit a large number of the mass murders.

Bible discussion questions:

1. Read Romans 5:1-8. What do you find comforting in these verses? Challenging?

2. Which one of the author's seven observations about Romans 5:1-8 stands out for you? Why?

3. Read 2 Corinthians 11:1-3 and John 3:1-18. Which verses in each passage impress you with God's truth the most? Please explain why.

4. Read Ephesians 4:20-24. What is your reaction to this passage and to the author's explanation of it in the context of both halves of Ephesians? How do these verses relate to our emotional marathon and this refreshment station? Explain.

5. Read 1 Thessalonians 5:23, 24. Which ones of the author's comments are useful to you as you run toward your finish-line of peace? Why?

6. Which of the people's sayings about anger are the most helpful to you? With which do you disagree? Why?

7. In looking back over this refreshment station, how does the author's distinction about the conscious, subconscious, and

unconscious help you understand your spiritual life? Why?

* * *

One Step On Our Journey With Jesus: Ask God persistently to enable you to decrease the intensity of your anger. Claim the victory of Jesus' death and resurrection to enable you to replace your anger with his love. Ask for his victory to understand lovingly people's actions rather than being tempted to react angrily. Pray persistently that God will replace your frustration with submission, your impatience with patience, and your other angry qualities with loving characteristics.

* * *

Refreshment Station 4: Get in touch with your anger and anxiety.

Struggles with uncovering our anger and anxiety
This "refreshment station" may be the hardest one of all for you, since uncovering events and people that have made us angry and/or

scared can be unsettling, to say the least. However, I'm convinced from personal experience and training that we need to face our personal "demons" in order to overcome them by Jesus' grace alone.

I know that God doesn't want us to harbor any past anger or anxiety because of his many promises of peace, not only the outer peace in relationship with him but also the inner kind within our conscious, subconscious, and unconscious minds.

As a result, how do we go about getting in touch with our anger and anxiety? First, we must test ourselves concerning our anger's intensity. I find that if my muscles, especially in my forehead, are getting tight, I know that I've let my anger level build up. Also, if I'm irritable or frustrated about little matters, my anger-meter has increased.

I'm convinced that our emotional life is like a tea kettle in which our steamy anger gradually grows with higher and higher pressure. We can choose to unload it in a sinful way on other people, hold it all in with unhealthy results, or let the valve of prayer lower our anger's pressure.

Monitor you own life to see if your anger's intensity is greater. If you can't determine it on your own, ask a trusted friend or your spouse if you are reacting intensely to less important events or situations.

Moreover, if you detect high intensity in your reactions to circumstances and can't figure out why you're angry or anxious in the present, then it's time to search your past, especially your childhood, to find out the root-cause of your anger.

Of course, we don't often want to face those issues, but God can help us as we go through our self-discovery.

Definitely ask God to reveal the root causes of your anger to you. I named my first book, *Doubtbusters! God Is My Shrink!* because he has been my Psychiatrist on more than one occasion and has used human mental-health professionals too.

No one has had perfect parents and families. We may have buried deep in our unconscious mind some action of a parent or relative that made us angry or scared that has accumulated with other causes to make us angry or anxious in the present. More than likely, one of our brothers or sisters treated us unlovingly more than once.

In prayer, persist in asking God to reveal those past events that affect your emotions now. If you can't discover the cause, you might seek a good therapist, preferably a Christian, who can be God's agent to help you uncover your feelings about your childhood and more recent past.

In my case, my first psychiatrist just listened to me and took my money for six months without any help. The second one had me do all of the psychological tests but misdiagnosed me as bipolar instead of having depression. It wasn't until I entered Pine Rest Christian Mental Hospital that God used the great psychological professionals there to make many breakthroughs in my therapy group and psychodrama. You can read about God's dramatic work in my life in *Doubtbusters!*

Anger and anxiety in the Old Testament
Anyway, God certainly wants us to face and overcome our anger and anxiety. In terms of

his reaction to our anger, you might consider God's confrontation of Cain's anger at his brother Abel in Genesis 4:6, 7: "Then the LORD said to Cain, 'Why are you angry? Why is your face downcast? If you do what is right, will you not be accepted? But if you do not do what is right, sin is crouching at your door; it desires to have you, but you must master it.'" God wants to give us Jesus' victory to face and decrease the intensity of our anger and anxiety so that we don't hurt others with our words and actions.

Of course, even though Cain's real issue was his unbelieving, defective worship and service, he took his angry reaction to God's loving confrontation out on his brother, Abel, by murdering him. To avoid hurting our loved ones, we need to master our anger when the real issue is our past. If we have hurt them already, we need to confess our unloving actions and words to them regardless of their reactions to our confession.

In terms of our fears or anxieties or worries, God has spoken the Ten Commandments to Israel with his own voice, not to whip them into shape in order to keep them in line with terror, as some belief systems try to do. In

Exodus 20:2, God said to them, "I am the LORD your God, who brought you out of Egypt, out of the land of slavery." In other words, the reason they need to obey God's laws is to express their thankfulness for God's rescue from Egyptian slavery, not their terror at his greatness.

However, the people's leaders come to Moses after their Mount Sinai experience to say, "Speak to us yourself and we will listen. But do not have God speak to us or we will die" (Exodus 20:19). Obviously, Israel reacts with terror and dread rather than thankful respect for God when he spoke his commands with his own voice.

Then, Moses uses the same word "fear" for the two kinds of fear in saying, "Do not be afraid. God has come to test you, so that the fear of God will be with you to keep you from sinning" (Exodus 20:20). We might say that Moses, at God's leading, has enabled our eyesight about fear to be 20/20!

I apologize for my attempt at humor. However, my point is that anxiety, the first kind in Moses' statement, that starts in our childhood is a terror or dread about certain events and actions by others.

On the other hand, believers' "fear of God," the second kind of fear, is a spiritually healthy awe and respect for our great Creator. It is a little like children's respect for their parents when they realize that the discipline results from their love for them.

Another Bible passage that describes God's help for a believer's fear, anger, and depression is 1 Kings 19:1-18. Elijah has just been God's agent for a great triumph over the false god Baal and that god's prophets on Mount Carmel (1 Kings 18:16-46). Then, Israel's Baal-worshiping Queen Jezebel "put a price on Elijah's head" instead of acknowledging that the true God of Israel was Yahweh.

From his high mountaintop experience, Elijah fell into the deep valley of depression and anxiety for his life. "Elijah was afraid and ran for his life [south into the desert toward Mount Sinai]. ...He came to a broom tree, sat down under it, and prayed that he might die. 'I have had enough, LORD,' he said. 'Take my life; I am no better than my ancestors'" (1

Kings 19:3a, 4b). Well, God wasn't ready to take Elijah's life; he still had errands to do for God.

I want to make the following point extremely clear: If you ever have suicidal thoughts and want to die like Elijah, get psychological help immediately to discover the real cause of your desires! If you can't overcome those desires, check yourself into a good Christian mental hospital like Pine Rest in Grand Rapids, Michigan, to get God's help!

In addition, if people relate any of their thoughts about suicide to you, even in a joking manner, talk to them about getting help, even if you have to use a family intervention. Their lives may depend on your actions.

With that urgent advice, I want you to notice God's amazing patience and love shown to Elijah, since he merely asks twice why Elijah has traveled to Sinai. He then lets Elijah complain twice about the supposed failure of his faithful, prophetic service for God; his assumption that he is the only person left who was faithful to the true God of Israel; and Jezebel's threat to kill him (verse 10 and 14).

God patiently listens to our complaints done in faith with our focus on him. We'll see that biblical fact again several times during another refreshment station later in this book.

Of course, God assures Elijah that 7,000 people are still faithful to him and gives him a couple more missions to do before he later goes up to heaven without dying, an astounding, miraculous event that is witnessed by Elijah's prophetic successor, Elisha (2 Kings 2).

Anger and anxiety in the New Testament
Furthermore, Jesus in his Sermon on the Mount deals with anger. In Matthew 5:21-26, he contrasts his teaching with the religious leaders' external application of God's command to avoid murder. "But I tell you that anyone who is angry with his brother will be subject to judgment." Jesus' astounding statement goes much deeper than the outward action of taking someone's life to the root of murder, self-centered anger.

We have all been guilty of such selfish anger. I remember once when my younger brother and I were watching TV, we argued about which show we should watch. As we rolled around the floor wrestling with each other over that decision, I remember wanting to kill him. Thankfully, God restrained us both. However, the desire and anger were enough to make me guilty of murder, according to Jesus.

The thought then occurs to me that if we are all guilty of murder as Jesus defined it, are we all on our way to hell? All believers know that the same Jesus who held us guilty has provided our escape from his own guilty verdict by suffering and dying in our place. The result is that through faith in him we receive God the Judge's not-guilty verdict. Jesus' amazing actions in believers' lives should be our loving, joyful, and thankful obedience to his Word as his adopted children.

Jesus also addresses our anxiety or worry about the future in his Sermon on the Mount. In Matthew 6:18-24, he says that God is our only treasure in this life and the next. Then, he commands us in verses 25, 27, and 33, "Therefore I tell you, do not worry about your life, what you will eat or drink; or about your body, what you will wear.... Who of you by worrying can add a single hour to his life?... For the pagans run after all these things, and your heavenly Father knows that you need them. But seek first his kingdom and his righteousness, and all these things will be given to you as well."

Islamic terrorism, spreading diseases, and many mass murders may make us angry and anxious. However, what's the worst that can happen to us? We could be victims of Muslim terrorism, a virus, or a mass murder; but if I died in such an attack, my soul would immediately be in Jesus' loving arms to await inhabiting my perfect resurrected body when he comes back. As Paul wrote, "For to me, to live is Christ and to die is gain" (Philippians 1:21).

Jesus' point in Matthew 6 is that God must be our most valued possession. If he is, we don't need to worry or let people terrorize or murder us.

We must not leave Paul out in our survey about anger and anxiety. In Ephesians 4:26, 27, 29-32, Paul frames his calls to Christian progress with his teaching about the Christian life as a process of taking off the old, selfish "clothes" of our old nature and putting on our God-centered "clothes."

He includes anger in those old-nature characteristics as follows: "'In your anger do not sin' [quoting Psalm 4:4]. Do not let the sun go down while you are still angry, and do not give the devil a foothold....Do not let any unwholesome talk come out of your mouths, but only what is helpful for building others up according to their needs, that it may benefit those who listen. and do not grieve the Holy Spirit of God, with whom you were sealed for the day of redemption. Get rid of all bitterness, rage, and anger, brawling and slander, along with every form of malice. Be kind and compassionate to one another, forgiving each other, just as in Christ God forgave you."

Several comments come to mind about this passage:

(1) Psalm 4, from which Paul quoted, has interesting verses about anger. It is one of David's many prayers for deliverance from his enemies. He says that there is anger without sinfulness. How can that be? Well, if our anger focuses on the people who wronged us, it usually involves sin because it's selfish. However, if our anger calls on God as the Judge who will justly declare all people guilty or not guilty, our ire is righteous indignation instead.

(2) Then, the fulfillment of Psalm 4:6-8 will happen, "Many are asking, 'Who can show us any good?' Let the light of your face shine upon us, O LORD. You have filled my heart with greater joy than when their grain and new wine abound. I will lie down and sleep in peace, for you alone, O LORD, make me dwell in safety." Joy and peace are God's gifts coming from an unselfish focus on God as the Source of justice and peace rather than on people, who will often disappoint us.

(3) Paul's call for a sunset deadline for our anger is, of course, not to be used legalistically; but his point is that we must not hold onto our anger at others' actions but must let God judge them. Of course, God obviously doesn't want us to bury our anger in our subconscious or unconscious mind, an action that wouldn't be letting go of it. He wants us to rely on him to overcome it instead.

(4) Notice that Paul couples harbored anger with giving "the devil a foothold." Satan wants us to get mired down in our anger's quicksand rather than giving it to God (more later in this book).

(5) "Unwholesome talk" can often come from our anger. One example can be spreading around a juicy story about someone without checking with that person to find out whether or not it's true. Our angry action of gossiping about or judging others may have been a reaction to some abuse or unloving actions that someone did to us in the past.

(6) Paul calls us to replace these old-nature actions with upbuilding words. He also says that all such old, sinful clothes that we keep wearing grieve the Holy Spirit. In uncovering and dealing with our anger and anxiety, we avoid making him grieve. (Those who say that the Holy Spirit is only a power of God, not a Person, have trouble explaining this verse, since we can't grieve a power!)

(7) In verses 31 and 32, Paul contrasts two more pieces of clothes, self-centered anger (verse 31) and God-centered kindness, compassion, and forgiveness that we receive through Jesus' life, death, and resurrection that result in God's forgiveness of our sins. We are reminded that Jesus taught us to pray, "Forgive us our debts as we forgive our debtors." If our anger and anxiety control us

so that we can't forgive others, we have little evidence that God has really forgiven us.

Another New Testament passage deals with anxiety. First Peter 5:6, 7 contains God's commands for his anxious children, "Humble yourselves, therefore, under God's mighty hand that he may lift you up in due time. Cast all your anxiety on him because he cares for you." Instead of letting other people like terrorists, murderers, diseases, and abusers control us through our worry and anxiety, God calls us to recognize that he rules even those angry people, as well as diseases, and that we don't. As a result, we must throw our anxiety at him. We will find out how to do that kind of "casting" as we continue our marathon.

A final verse, Hebrews 12:15, is among several calls in that chapter for Christians to make spiritual progress, "See to it that no one misses the grace of God and that no bitter root grows up to cause trouble and defile many." Our unconscious lives contain many roots that began in our childhoods. Bitterness or deep-seated anger grows up unless we pull it up by its roots.

I tried to find jokes about anger to lighten up my book but failed. I only have sayings about anger that reinforce or contrast with the biblical truths in this book:

"Life is so short. The only person you hurt when you stay angry or hold grudges is you. Forgive everyone, including yourself."—Tom Giaquinto

"I came to realize that if people could make me angry, they could control me. Why should I give someone else such power over my life?"—Ben Carson, *Gifted Hands: The Ben Carson Story*

"Anger does not solve anything; it builds nothing."—Thomas S. Monson

"When you look at the past without God's eyes, you subject yourself to deception.
The past no longer exists, and God doesn't linger there. However, Satan will show you whatever you want to see and believe, so you will be trapped in an emotion that cannot communicate truth, beyond what you want to remember."—Shannon L. Alder

Bible discussion questions:

(1) What is your overall reaction to the section "Struggles with uncovering our anger and anxiety"? Why do you react that way?

(2) Read Genesis 4:6, 7 and 1 Kings 19:1-18. How do you feel about God's two different responses to Cain and Elijah's anger? Explain.

(3) Read Exodus 20:1-20. Explain in your own words the two kinds of fear in verses 19 and 20. How can we be God-fearers in the best biblical sense? Explain.

(4) Read Matthew 5:18-24 and 6:18-33. What kind of anger and anxiety does Jesus call us to avoid? How can we overcome both? Explain.

(5) Read Ephesians 4:20—5:2. How can we practically take off the old-nature "clothes" and put on the new-nature "clothes"? Which verses tell us the key to such activity so that we can be more successful than many people's New Year's resolutions are? Which ones of the author's comments resonate the most in your mind? Why?

(6) Read 1 Peter 5:6, 7 and Hebrews 12:15. What is your reaction? Why do you feel that way? Which of the four quotations is the most important for your emotional life? Why?

* * *

One Step On Our Journey With Jesus: Set aside some time to pray persistently to God for his help as you take inventory of your emotions, especially your emotional reactions, including your irritation and worry, about people and events in your life. Ask your divine "Shrink" to help you take an objective inventory of the times when you react angrily to comparatively unimportant matters. Write them down in a journal and ask God to search your past, especially your childhood, for the root causes of your reactions to present circumstances. If your persistent prayers don't yield any causes, pray for God's guidance about your next steps. Keep your list for a future refreshment station.

* * *

Refreshment station 5: Acknowledge your grief.

You've probably heard about Elizabeth Kubler-Ross' five stages of grief: denial, anger, bargaining, depression, and acceptance. Notice that two of those stages are anger and depression, the second of which I believe to be, in many cases, anger turned inward. She found these in all patients, whether they were Christians or not. My point here is that we have all had losses, small or big, that have caused us to be angry in a greater or lesser degree.

Perhaps, when you were a child, a pet died, your parents favored other children over you, or you had your heart set on getting a certain present for Christmas. I remember that I saw a shiny, red bicycle in the hardware window. I prayed for months that God would guide my parents to give me that fancy bike. When God said no to my prayer, I decided that praying was useless and that I would ignore him until God grabbed onto me at the age of sixteen.

My point is that I was angry at God for saying no to my prayer. My problem was that I assumed that God was a Santa Claus in the sky. He had to teach me that his gifts are all free, not at all earned, and that prayer wasn't like a smash-and-grab jewelry-store robbery, when God is going give everything we want to have.

Most of us have unresolved issues with our brothers and/or sisters. As a pastor, I have seen such buried, unconscious issues come back at the death of a parent, especially the second parent.

How does God want us to deal with and overcome our grief and not get stuck in it? The answer will be our reward for our perseverance in continuing on to the remaining refreshment stations. However, at this station, we need to acknowledge our grief, especially the anger and often-accompanying anxiety that we often feel.

Human grief in the Old Testament

God's response to human grief is amazing. For example, in Genesis 21, after the miraculous birth of Isaac, Abraham and Sarah had an argument about what to do with their son Ishmael and his mother, Hagar, the slave woman with whom Abraham had the child outside of God's will to fulfill the promise of a male heir.

Sarah told Abraham to eject Hagar and Ishmael from the family to get rid of the expected rivalry. He reluctantly agrees when God assures him that he would take care of them. In the desert, they run out of water and bread. Then, Hagar leaves Ishmael because she can't bear to see him die. "And as she sat there nearby, she began to sob. God heard the boy crying, and the angel of God called to Hagar from heaven and said to her, 'What is the matter, Hagar? Do not be afraid; God has heard the boy crying as he lies there. Lift the boy up and take him by the hand, for I will make him into a great nation.'" (verses 16b-18).

Even though Hagar is only a slave and God has rejected Ishmael as Abraham's covenant child, God still responds in love to their expressed grief. How much more will he show his great love to his followers when we express anger and anxiety to him in prayer!

Another passage shows that God responds to believers' prayers when they pray to him in the anguish of their sorrow. In 1 Samuel 1, Elkanah has two wives, a prescription for possible marital disaster. God has blessed his wife Peninnah with children but has withheld that blessing from the other wife, Hannah. Sadly, Peninnah "provoked [Hannah] til she wept and would not eat....Once when they had finished eating and drinking in Shiloh,

Hannah stood up. Now Eli the priest was sitting on a chair by the doorpost of the LORD's temple [tabernacle]. In bitterness of soul Hannah wept much and prayed to the LORD....As she kept on praying to the LORD, Eli observed her mouth [and jumped to the conclusion that she was drunk]....[She answered him,] 'I have been praying here out of my great anguish and grief.' Eli answered, 'Go in peace, and may the God of Israel grant you what you have asked of him'" (verses 7b, 9, 10, 12, 15-17). God's comfort through the priest Eli's words gives her real hopeful joy.

Notice that God answers Hagar's grief expressed in weeping; while he answers Hannah's passionate, grieving prayers for a son whom she promises to dedicate to God's service at the place of worship. No wonder God gives Isaiah's future Messiah the name "Wonderful Counselor" (Isaiah 9:6)! Jesus certainly is our prayer-hearer!

So that we don't fall into the trap of many people's ideas that God is entirely-distant and unfeeling, we must listen to another prophecy that Jesus fulfills, Isaiah 53:3a, 4: "He was despised and rejected by men, a man of sorrows, and familiar with suffering....Surely he took up our infirmities and carried our sorrows, yet we considered him stricken by God, smitten by him, and afflicted."

Just feel these verses. The Second Person of the Creator-God joins the human race while remaining God, as he has claimed, in order to identify with our grief and carry it to the suffocating suffering of the Romans' most horrifying torture on a criminal's cross. No matter what severe losses and unloving actions you have suffered, Jesus has suffered more severely.

However, he has suffered in order to heal our grief. Never forget that fact. Isaiah 53:11 prophesies Jesus' victory for us who grieve, "After the suffering of his soul, he will see the light of life and be satisfied; by his knowledge my righteous servant will justify many, and he will bear their iniquities." His permanent resurrection on the third day confirms his followers' victory over our suffering and grief, including our anger and depression.

On the other hand, some depression involves disrupted brain chemicals and must be treated with medications for the rest of the patient's life.

According to God's Word, temporary victory can happen in this life to replace our anger and anxiety with his peace that transcends understanding (Philippians 4:6, 7). What's more, our experience of Jesus' triumph will be full and perfect when Jesus returns.

Another Old Testament passage about suffering and grief involves Jeremiah's lament over Jerusalem's extreme suffering at being exiled from God's Promised Land to Babylon (Lamentations 1:10, 11), "The enemy laid hands on all her treasures; she saw pagan nations enter her sanctuary—those you had forbidden to enter your assembly. All her people groan as they search for bread; they barter their treasures for food to keep themselves alive. 'Look, O LORD, and consider, for I am despised.'"

Grief and suffering involve our reaction to the differences between our present or past circumstance and the blessings that God has promised us in the Bible. Judah, God's people, has received God's promise of peace and rest in the Promised Land; and God has blessed them with a central place of worship, the tabernacle and later Solomon's temple.

Within that sacred place, only the priests were able to enter and perform the animal sacrifices that look forward to Jesus' one-time sacrifice on the cross.

God has only permitted the High Priest to enter the inner sanctuary, the Most Holy Place, once a year to sprinkle the blood of the sacrifices. That entrance is God's picture that he only recognizes the shedding of blood to forgive the people's rebellion in their personal and group lives.

Our grief comes with the often-vast difference between our circumstances and God's promises of overflowing blessings in our lives as believers. Jeremiah feels that great contrast and points out to God that he has allowed even the pagan unbelievers to enter the Most Holy Place and has permitted his people to become begging poor!

Of course, Judah's suffering has also happened because his people have worshiped and served false gods alongside of or instead of the only true God, who was amazingly patient with them until his patience ended when he ejected them from his land.

In our case, if our suffering has happened because of people's unloving actions or words, they are responsible to the God of the universe for their actions and will be accountable to him at the future Final Judgment. What a comfort that final day is to me that when other people treat me with unloving actions or words, God will judge them. Isn't that fact a comfort to you too?

However, God also made it clear in his Word that we are to express our grieving feelings about our suffering to him in prayer, just as Jeremiah does in Lamentations. We will return to that often-neglected book at another refreshment station.

Human grief in the New Testament
In a familiar verse in the New Testament, Matthew 5:4, Jesus says, "Blessed are those who mourn, for they will be comforted." In western cultures, we tend to repress our grief to avoid mourning. The English have the "stiff upper lip"; and other cultures, at least in the West, bury grief, at least publicly. In other words, when was the last time you saw someone have a good, unashamed cry?

We men have the tendency to think that crying is a sign of weakness, but shedding tears is a natural, stress-relieving action. We will see more about that expression of our grief later.

I've shared this experience at one other place, but it fits here. When I was about five years old, I was tricycling around our tennis court behind our house when I fell off my tricycle. (I've always been a klutz.)

I lay on the concrete bawling when my mom came out of the house. She picked me up, dusted me off, and said those unhealthy words from the American culture, "Big boys don't cry."

Well, I took those words to heart and buried my anger and anxiety in my unconscious minds, an action that resulted much later in seven years of major depression.

Here, we need to distinguish between grieving and mourning. Jesus says that God's blessing comes to mourners. Grieving is our inner reaction to our losses, while mourning involves our outward actions that express our inner grief. Of course, we need to grieve and mourn God's way, about which we will see more as we run our race.

Jesus' promise is that God will comfort our inner grief. His promise is the subject of this book as we run our emotional marathon.

The important observation that I make at this point is that we need to get in touch with our inner grief in our unconscious minds in order to receive God's comfort for our mourning.

The people of the Middle Eastern culture out of which the Bible came is much freer in terms of expressing grief in outward mourning. That culture is much healthier than the West's by more-freely expressing grief in their mourning. I've seen news videos in Turkey, for example, of people wailing their losses in earthquakes and other disasters. Crying is beneficial, as we will see.

Another verse is the shortest one in the Bible, "Jesus wept" (John 11:35). How could Jesus weep? After all, wasn't he God? Yes, he was fully God, but he was also completely human.

Jesus arrives at Mary and Martha's home four days after Lazarus has died. It seems to them that he can't help Lazarus any more. A large crowd of mourners cries openly about his death. Many of them question why Jesus has been that tardy, since they have seen his many healings. They ask, "Could not he who opened the eyes of the blind man [John 9] have kept this man from dying?" (John 11:37).

We know that Jesus is about to resuscitate Lazarus. Why, then, did he weep? One reason in the text is that he mourns the people's unbelief, because after he raises the young man, they report his actions to the religious leaders. His amazing miracle is the turning point in John's gospel that eventually leads to Jesus' death.

Also, not only does Jesus mourn the people's unbelief, but he also weeps in sympathy with Martha and Mary over their loss of their brother, even though he knows that he is going to bring him back to life. Yes, Jesus sympathizes with our grief enough to carry it to the cross and from his empty tomb. The result is that he releases unlimited divine power in those events to replace our anger and anxiety with his lasting peace.

My point is that when we grieve, Jesus weeps with us!

At any rate, later, Jesus revealed to his followers that he would be leaving them (John 13:31-33). Understandably, they felt grief at his words because they, like most of the Jews, wanted him to be an earthly, political Messiah that would liberate them from cruel Roman domination.

In reply to their grief, he said the following familiar words, "Do not let your hearts be troubled. Trust in God, trust also in me. In my Father's house are many rooms. If it were not so, I would have told you. I am going there to prepare a place for you. And if I go and prepare a place for you, I will come back and take you to be with me that you also may be where I am....I am the way and the truth and the life. No one comes to the Father except through me" (John 14:1-3, 6). Jesus' comforting words prompt several comments:

(1) Many believers in the face of death's reality and in other times of suffering have received God's great and gracious comfort through these words of Jesus.

(2) Jesus did not tell us to bury our grief in our unconscious minds but to receive God's comforting peace to replace it. Such comfort must begin with trust in God the Father and in Jesus.

(3) Many people today think that all belief systems are merely different ways we can get to God's acceptance. In my experience, a high school teacher, a native American, and an older neighbor all believed this lie of the evil one. Jesus clearly contradicted that idea by saying that he came from the Father, would return to him, and would return as the only one who will usher us into his perfect presence.

(4) Moreover, in response to the disciples' ignorance, he clearly said that he, the Prince of Peace, was the only Pathway to God and his gift of peace as well as being the only truth and the only Source of eternal life, one of John's favorite themes.

(5) He provided more than one fulfillment of his promise to come back to take his followers to his Father's heavenly palace. After his resurrection, he appeared to them several times. At their deaths, most of them because

of persecution, he took them home. When we believers die, he takes our souls to his Father's palace.

(6) When he will return to us who are still alive at his coming with the souls of believers who have died, he will reunite our perfected bodies with our souls finally to enter God's heavenly palace, which I believe will be the new universe that John described in Revelation 21:1-4.

(7) Come soon, Lord Jesus, to replace our grief and mourning with your final, perfect peace!

Furthermore, in 1 Thessalonians 4:13, Paul addressed the people's grief by making a distinction between that of unbelievers and believers. He wrote, "Brothers, we do not want you to be ignorant about those who fall asleep [die] or to grieve like the rest of men, who have no hope." He then went on to describe Jesus' Second Coming as the future event that gives believers profound hope and comfort.

Notice, however, that Paul did not say that we are not to grieve but that we are to grieve with hope of Jesus' return. Apparently, some of the Thessalonians had quit their jobs in order to await that future event about which Paul had preached. He wrote to correct their mistaken actions.

They also worried that their loved ones who had died since Paul preached in Thessalonica would lose out on Jesus' coming. In the following passage, he made clear that Jesus will bring their loved ones' souls back with him to participate in the ensuing resurrection of all people for the Final Judgment.

* * *

I found a list of forty ways to achieve peace of mind at lifehack.com. Many of them are good suggestions similar to God's suggestions, but they are all humanistic ways to achieve temporary peace, which is the human way, not the godly way. Instead, I am pointing you to God's permanent peace.

* * *

At this point, we need to ask where in the New Testament we can find commands to grieve and mourn about our actions and those of others. Well, James 4:7-10 has ten commands for Christians to move from their self-centered sin to God's inner peace. I quote and comment on those verses: "Submit yourselves, then, to God. Resist the devil, and he will flee from you. Come near to God, and he will come near to you. Wash your hands, you sinners, and purify your hearts, you double-minded. Grieve, mourn, and wail. Change your laughter to mourning and your joy to gloom. Humble yourselves before the Lord, and he will lift you up."

(1) In the rest of the chapter before and after these verses, James calls us to overcome self-centered disputes (verses 1-3), friendship with the human culture around us (verses 4-6), spreading around falsehoods about others to make ourselves seem good (verses 11,12), and selfish plans that we fail to submit to God's will (verses 13-17).

(2) Thus, James' ten inspired commands call believers to move more and more from selfish living to God-centered lives.

(3) Our grieving of past events and people sometimes denies that we had any responsibility at all. We would be right if

adults abused us emotionally, physically, and/or sexually. However, our self-centered sin shows itself when we hold on to our anger at the people who abused or treated us unlovingly.

(4) Our unconscious minds can let our anger and grief increase to the boiling point when they move into our conscious minds. If we can't let go of our anger and, as a result, let God judge them, our self-centered anger festers like a sliver that someone must take out. God wants to remove it for us.

(5) Therefore, since the devil wants us to wallow in our angry mud-bath like a hog, God commands us to resist Satan by grieving, mourning, and wailing about our past and present that cause us to grieve. We also need to mourn about our sinfulness when we have bitterly held onto our grudges about the people in our past.

(6) James does not call us to walk around all of the time with our chins dragging on the ground. However, if we tend to cover our grief up with a smile—the way I did for the first forty-three years of my life to cover up my unconscious anger and grief at my

losses—then we need to uncover our grief in order to express it honestly to him in prayer. We will see many more biblical examples of such mentally healthy expressions in succeeding refreshment stations.

(7) The key command for our peace progress is James' call for us to humble ourselves before God. When we set ourselves up as the judge of our abusers, enemies, and of God himself for allowing those events to take place, we take God's rightful place as his creation's Judge. That sin belonged to Adam and Eve and all of humanity since then. We all have tried to raise ourselves to God's level by pronouncing our judgments against other people, but we need him to lower us to our proper status as his lowly creatures instead.

(8) However, notice God's promise through James that when we let go of our high judicial status and lower ourselves to let him judge others, he will lift us up. In our case, we will see that God wants to give us inner peace.

Read the following sayings as God's observations through four different people: "Anger does not solve anything; it builds nothing."—Thomas S. Monson,

"When you look at the past without God's eyes, you subject yourself to deception. The past no longer exists and God doesn't linger there. However, Satan will show you whatever you want to see and believe, so you will be trapped in an emotion that cannot communicate truth, beyond what you want to remember."—Shannon L. Alder,

"If you're angry at a loved one, hug that person. And mean it. You may not want to hug - which is all the more reason to do so. It's hard to stay angry when someone shows they love you, and that's precisely what happens when we hug each other."—Walter Anderson, *The Confidence Course: Seven Steps to Self-Fulfillment,*

"Anger is the wind which blows out the lamp of the mind."—Bodie Thoene.

Bible discussion questions:

(1) Read Genesis 21:1-21. What verses stand out in your mind? Describe in your own words God's actions toward Hagar and Ishmael, the non-heir in Abraham's family tree? Why does God choose Isaac instead of Ishmael, through whom he would bless Abraham's descendants leading to Jesus? Explain.

(2) Read 1 Samuel 1:1-20. How does God respond to Hannah's anguished, persistent prayers? Why do you think he gave her Samuel? What verses stand out in your mind? Why?

(3) What does the Messiah's title in Isaiah 9:6 "Wonderful Counselor" mean to you? What does Jesus have to do with our grief? How is that title related to another title "Prince of Peace"? Explain.

(4) Read John 11:1-46. What do you think about the author's explanation of verse 37? What does Jesus' weeping have to do with our grief? Explain.

(5) Read John 13:31—14:6. Why does Jesus have to comfort his followers? How are his words a comfort to us in our times of grief? Why?

(6) Read 1 Thessalonians 4:13-18. What does Paul say about his readers' grief? How are his words a great comfort to us in our grief? Explain.

(7) Read James 4:7-10. Why does James command us to "grieve, mourn, and wail"?

How can we practically obey his ten commands? Explain.

(8) Which one of the four sayings is the most meaningful to you? Why?

* * *

A Step On Our Journey With Jesus: Ask God persistently in prayer what past events you are angry or grieving about. Also, pray that he will take away your self-centered judgment and that he will enable you to let him be the Judge of the people who have hurt you.

* * *

Life's Emotional Marathon Part III: **Pursue the prayerful Pathway to inner peace.**

Refreshment station 6: **Understand depression.**

Many people understand anger to be equal to strong displeasure in reaction to a perceived wrong. Dictionaries even define the word "anger" that way. However, they merely reflect common usage.

On the other hand, the emotion really involves a desire to attack or oppose the source of the displeasure. It can range from a minor irritation to frustration to resentment to bitterness to uncontrolled rage.

Since we are born with self-centered anger that is often shown in our emotional response to being outside of the womb, we often bury it in our unconscious minds in order to please other people. Anger builds up over time and will show up at times when we least expect it.

I don't agree with Sigmund Freud on much of his personality theory except for his statement that depression is anger turned inward. Why? I agree because of my own experience.

From 1979 to 1986, I experienced deepening, major depression. I sought a physical cause for my increasing fatigue but found no medical reason for it. Finally, after I had two severe anxiety attacks a week apart and an emotional shutdown, I went to two different psychiatrists with no help. Then, I entered

Pine Rest Mental Health Hospital in Grand Rapids, Michigan.

I won't detail the dramatic events that God used to get me in touch with my unconscious anger. (You can read about them in my first book, *Doubtbusters! God Is My Shrink!*) God's almost-miraculous result was the process that I share with you during the remaining refreshment stations. Believe me when I tell you that Sigmund Freud was right about the unconscious mind storing up anger to produce depression. The other result can be rage, which we definitely don't want to happen because it will hurt other people.

Bible passages showing human and divine anger

People's anger is often focused on other people's actions. In Numbers 20:1-13, the people of Israel quarrel with Moses and Aaron because of their lack of water. Note that they don't pray to God but complain, instead, to their earthly leaders. They focus on people rather than on the LORD, a common way for unbelievers to react to their lack of basic needs.

Then, God gives Moses and Aaron specific directions to follow in satisfying the people's thirst. They must take Moses' staff with which God opened the Rea Sea, go to a certain boulder, and speak to it. It sounds simple.

However, Moses is so frustrated with the people's grumbling rebellion that he pounds the rock with his staff instead of speaking to it. In spite of Moses and Aaron's disobedience, God delivers gushing fresh water from the rock but denies them the opportunity to enter the Promised Land because of their disobedience. The point is that self-centered anger brings consequences, even though God is very patient.

By contrast, notice Moses' God-centered anger on Mount Sinai. At that time, he breaks the two tablets of the Ten Commandments written by God when the people are worshiping the golden calf-god after their impatience with Moses' forty-day visit with God on Mt. Sinai (Exodus 32). Interestingly, Moses' anger at the Israelites then turns into prayer for them when God's just anger burns against them.

God's summarized solution for our anger and depression

Then, how can we deal with the troubles we experience in this life? The rest of this book and your marathon will explain the pathway to peace. However, Jesus summarizes his gift in one of his last promises to his closest followers in this way (John 16:33), "I have told you these things, so that in me you may have peace. In this world you will have trouble. But take heart! I have overcome the world." Notice that Jesus' gift of peace comes through his words, which he has inspired the Bible's writers to put on parchment and that he has preserved for our instruction.

Observe in Jesus' words that no matter what circumstances give us anger and anxiety, Jesus has already overcome them because he has defeated Satan and his followers in principle and wants to defeat them in practice in our lives. That triumphant process is the subject of our remaining refreshment stations as we persevere.

Also, in Romans 8, that enormously comforting chapter, the Apostle summarizes our situation in God's creation (verses 22-26):

22 We know that the whole creation has been

groaning as in the pains of childbirth right up to the present time. 23 Not only so, but we ourselves, who have the first fruits of the Spirit, groan inwardly as we wait eagerly for our adoption to sonship, the redemption of our bodies. 24 For in this hope we were saved. But hope that is seen is no hope at all. Who hopes for what they already have? 25 But if we hope for what we do not yet have, we wait for it patiently. 26 In the same way, the Spirit helps us in our weakness. We do not know what we ought to pray for, but the Spirit himself intercedes for us through wordless groans.

Absorb Paul's teachings in these verses:

(1) He compares the universe to a woman in labor. They have in common the fact that creation is in pain. We who feel anger and anxiety about our lives can identify with Paul's words in verse 22.

(2) Not only does the creation groan, but also Christians do along with the universe (verse 23). We have God's down payment on our future inheritance with God's gift of the Holy Spirit. The result is an eager hope for our final adoption to be inheritors ("sonship") that will be the "redemption of our bodies." Obviously, when Jesus returns, he will raise our perfected bodies to eternal life that we will live in his

new universe. We are also like women in labor because we groan because of pain with hope for his return.

(3) Depression can sap the hope out of our lives. However, as true Christians, we have hope for Jesus' second coming and our bodies' perfection. Paul's statement that God saves us in this hope means that hopeless depression, even an occasional down-in-the-dumps feeling, doesn't need to control us.

(4) In the meantime, God wants to give us relief from depression about each event that makes us angry and anxious, except for the one that is caused by chemicals in the brain. However, the result of hope is enduring patience (the end of verse 25).

(5) In John 16:33, we have seen that the Pathway to peace is Jesus' victory; but in verse 26, the Holy Spirit is also our Helper in the middle of our weakness through prayer. He cleans up our prayers to be presented to our heavenly Father. What a Comforter we have in the middle of our anger and anxiety!

Here is some anger-humor for your pleasure:

A golfer became so mad that he threw his brand-new set of golf clubs into the lake.
A few minutes later he came back, waded into the lake, and retrieved his clubs.
He proceeded to take his car keys out of the bag -- then threw the clubs back into the water.
(reallyshortfunnyjokes.com)

Anger as an emotion is without much reason, as this joke shows. You would think that he would have retrieved his golf clubs too, but they were a little less expensive than his car.

* * *

<u>Bible discussion questions:</u>

(1) Explain in your own words the difference between outer and inner peace. How do you feel about the difference? Why? Look at Romans 3:23 and 5:1-2. How does Paul describe outer peace? Explain. Also, read Philippians 4:4-7. How is this peace different? What makes it different? Why?

(2) What is your definition of the word "anger"? How does it compare with the author's definition? The dictionary's? Why do you think there are differences? (The author's definition comes from his experiences with

and learning about psychological issues.)
Explain.

(3) Read Exodus 32 and Numbers 20:1-13.
Describe God's, Moses', and Israel's anger.
How do you think we can move from self-
centered anger to God-centered anger? In
what ways are those two emotions different?
Explain.

(4) Read John 16:33. Why does Jesus say that
he has overcome the world's trouble? How?
How comforting is his statement to you?

(5) Read Romans 8:22-26 in the context of the
whole chapter. Tell the rest of the group how
this passage comforts you.

* * *

Refreshment Station 7: **Experience tears and hope.**

My combination of tears and hope seems to
be a contradiction, but we can have both grief
and expectation of a better future.

Tears

First, let's look at the Bible's references to people crying tears expressing their grief. Psalm 6 demonstrates the Bible's culture with its freedom of unloading tears that express grief:

1 LORD, do not rebuke me in your anger
or discipline me in your wrath.
2 Have mercy on me, LORD, for I am faint;
heal me, LORD, for my bones are in agony.
3 My soul is in deep anguish.
How long, LORD, how long?
4 Turn, LORD, and deliver me;
save me because of your unfailing love.
5 Among the dead no one proclaims your
name.
Who praises you from the grave?
6 I am worn out from my groaning.
All night long I flood my bed with weeping
and drench my couch with tears.
7 My eyes grow weak with sorrow;
they fail because of all my foes.
8 Away from me, all you who do evil,
for the LORD has heard my weeping.
9 The LORD has heard my cry for mercy;
the LORD accepts my prayer.

10 All my enemies will be overwhelmed with shame and anguish;
they will turn back and suddenly be put to shame.

King David's life is in danger. His enemies surround him as in Psalm 22. You can almost feel his passionate desperation. God seems to have deserted him. He cries tears of despair until verse 8, when he senses that God will come to his rescue.

The western culture suppresses tears even at funerals and covers them up at memorial services in my experience of twenty-seven years as a pastor leading those events. Why?

I believe that the reason is human pride, which equates tears with weakness. For example, as I told you above, my mother taught me, "Big boys don't cry," directly from the American culture. Also, we hear some people say that when other people cry, they "break down" in tears. Crying is not a breakdown; it's natural. In fact, mental illness doesn't have anything to do with a "nervous breakdown." Our nerves do not break down when we are afflicted with depression.

I'm afraid that I swallowed that teaching and my tears for the first thirty-six years of my life until I experienced seven years of deepening depression, a period of symptoms, primarily fatigue, caused by my anger turned inward, as Freud put it. In fact, since I didn't know that I was angry, it was deeply buried in my unconscious mind.

I'm a 6'4" man, but I'm not at all ashamed to say that God taught me to cry many tears when no human presented those teachings. I praise him to this day that he broke through to me to enable me to cry tearfully like David about stressful events and losses and find God's relief in the peace of Philippians 4:6-7, which has lasted over three decades. The result is that God has enabled me to accept those losses, even the death of our second child.

Another example of a psalmist's tears is Psalm 119:136, "Streams of tears flow from my eyes,
for your law is not obeyed." The writer laments about his people's neglect of obedience to God's rules. We can do the same kind of grieving over some churches' straying

from God's guidelines found in his inspired Word.

A third example is the Prophet Jeremiah's great grief over the exile of God's people from the promised land to Babylon (Lamentations 3:48-51),

48 Streams of tears flow from my eyes
because my people are destroyed.
49 My eyes will flow unceasingly,
without relief,
50 until the LORD looks down
from heaven and sees.
51 What I see brings grief to my soul
because of all the women of my city.

Some people might object that tearful lamenting happens in the writers' culture but doesn't often in ours. Therefore, they say we can disregard their crying as a pattern we don't need to follow.

However, God also reveals through science that emotional tears are healthy in a *Psychology Today* article entitled "The Health Benefits of Tears" by a medical doctor. She reveals that when our eyes water, those tears are 98% water. On the other hand, emotional tears have several more beneficial substances.

Therefore, she rejects our culture's frowning on shedding tears.

Dr. Judith Orloff states in that article, "Try to let go of outmoded, untrue conceptions about crying. It is good to cry. It is healthy to cry. This helps to emotionally clear sadness and stress. Crying is also essential to resolve grief, when waves of tears periodically come over us after we experience a loss. Tears help us process the loss so we can keep living with open hearts. Otherwise, we are a set up for *depression* if we suppress these potent feelings."

The great increase of depression in the western world could be prevented with tearful crying. More so, we Christians can greatly benefit from the examples of David and Jeremiah and the advice of Dr. Orloff.

A fourth and final example is Jesus himself in Luke 19:41-44, 41 As he approached Jerusalem and saw the city, he wept over it 42 and said, 'If you, even you, had only known on this day what would bring you peace—but now it is hidden from your eyes. 43 The days will come upon you when your enemies will build an embankment against you and encircle you and hem you in on every side. 44 They will dash you to the ground, you and the children within your walls. They will not leave one stone on another, because you did not recognize the time of God's coming to you.'"

Even though many people in the Christian church neglect this part of the Palm Sunday message, perhaps because it doesn't fit our emotionally-repressed western culture and experiences, I will not leave it alone by sharing the following comments:

(1) When Jesus weeps as he approaches Jerusalem, the word for "wept" in verse 41 describes loud wailing, unlike the quiet weeping that he did at Lazarus' grave in John 11:36.

(2) The majority of Jerusalem's population have hardened their hearts by attempting to follow the law and many other regulations in order to manipulate God into loving them without realizing that he has loved us long before we can do anything to earn it. Such willful blindness is very sad. Therefore, they don't recognize that the second Person of God, whose title is Prince of Peace (Isaiah 9:6) is among them (verse 42).

(3) The incredibly horrible result will be that the Romans will surround, ransack, and burn the city and temple (verses 43-44). The Romans will fulfill Jesus' prophecy literally forty years later in A.D. 70.

(4) The temple's gold wall- and furniture-coverings will melt in the intense heat, resulting in the Roman army taking all the temple's huge stones apart to get at the gold between the cracks (verse 44b).

(5) Thus, Jesus illustrates the incredible sadness of unbelieving resistance to God by humanity's majority. He also points to the amazing power that God uses to break through that lack of faith to rescue unbelievers to become true Christians as his followers.

<u>Bible discussion questions:</u>

(1) What do you think about the author's combination of tears and hope in his title of this refreshment station? How can he put those two ideas together? Explain your answer.

(2) What parts of our culture should we accept, and which should we reject in terms of our handling of emotions? Should we accept or reject the western culture's repression of tears and crying in grief? Why or why not?

(3) Read Psalm 6. Why did David, a macho man of war, shed tears? What was the result of his experience of grieving (see verses 8-10)? Why do you suppose David experienced this change to hope from tears? Explain.

(4) In Psalm 119:136, why does the psalmist weep tears of grief? What in God's church might cause a similar reaction in us? Why?

(5) Compare Dr. Orloff's recommendations about tearful crying and the author's similar experiences. How much will Christians be willing to follow their advice? Why?

(6) Read Luke 19:41-44. Why did Jesus wail loudly on Palm Sunday? Which one of the author's comments about those verses stands out most in your mind? Explain.

* * *

<u>One Step on our Journey with Jesus</u>: If you have trouble crying about the losses in your life or about your own sins, find a close friend or two with whom to do your devotions using this refreshment station. Share your feelings about your losses and sins in agreement that you won't share outside the group. As you gain mutual trust, give each other the permission to shed tears about the past and present. Show God's unconditional love through your expressions of support and your prayers for each other.

* * *

Hope
As you notice in looking back at Psalm 6:8-10, David suddenly finds hopeful expectation in the middle of his tears.

Another example of tears and hope is the Apostle Paul's instruction in 1 Thessalonians 4:13-18. Some people in the church in Thessalonica are scared that their loved ones who have died since Paul preached about Jesus' return will miss out on the resurrection.

He writes that passage to assure them that their souls will return with Jesus when he comes back to be raised with his readers' bodies. They won't miss all believers' bodily resurrection at Jesus' second coming. In verse 13, he writes to comfort them and us, "we do not want you to be uninformed about those who sleep in death, so that you do not grieve like the rest of mankind, who have no hope." In other words, Jesus' return means that when we grieve, we believers mourn with hope of Jesus' future resurrection of our bodies and those of our loved ones (see 1 Corinthians 15).

Sadly, unbelievers have no hope for the future of their loved ones in the middle of grief about their deaths.

Two of Jesus' beatitudes that combine believers' actions with God's blessings are relevant to our study at this point (Matthew 5:4, 5, 8):

4 Blessed are those who mourn,
for they will be comforted.
5 Blessed are the meek,
for they will inherit the earth….
8 Blessed are the pure in heart,
for they will see God.

Notice the following points:

(1) When we mourn persistently (verse 4)—as the original word's form implies, since it's in the present tense—God will enable us to have his peace from our anger and anxiety.

(2) To which of God's blessings do you look forward more, seeing God (verse 8) or inheriting the earth (verse 5)? I want to see the Father, Jesus, and the Holy Spirit as the one only true God. I can't see him now because I drag around with me this old, failing body. However, then I will have this body renewed and perfected without pain!

(3) What does "inheriting the earth" mean? Many people expect to flit off permanently to a spiritual place called heaven. Such a place does, indeed, exist; it's the place where God rules now.

(4) However, even though our souls will inhabit heaven after we die, when Jesus comes back, our souls will accompany him to rejoin our perfected resurrection bodies.

(5) At the same time, he will re-create this crumbling, decaying universe into a new heavens and new earth (Revelation 21:1). In that chapter and the following one, the new Jerusalem, a figurative picture of the perfected Old and New Testament people of God, comes down from heaven to the new earth, where our inheritance will be secure for eternity.

(6) What will we do forever? Well, the only tiny glimpse of our activities is the verb "reign" in the book of Revelation. What our job description will be under the heading "reigning," I have no idea because the Bible doesn't say.

(7) However, Adam and Eve have had the job of taking care of the garden of Eden. I assume that such activities on the new earth will involve our managing that new world.

(8) I need to make one last comment. In verse 8, the "pure in heart" will see God. Who are they? Jesus' substitution on the Roman torture tree for all true believers has made us all completely pure in God the Judge's sight.

(9) On the other hand, we must still overcome the impurity of our sinful natures remaining in us by the cleansing power of Jesus' death. When our earthly life has ended at our death or when Jesus returns, we will be completely pure and thus able to see God's "face" (Revelation 22:4).

(10) How eager are you for Jesus' predictions in his beatitudes to come true?

This combination of crying and hope is an example of the gospel's "already/not-yet" truths. I mean that much of the New Testament talks about what Jesus has accomplished in his life, death, and resurrection as well as what he does in believers' lives until they die.

For example, Jesus has "already" given us permanent outer peace with God (Romans 5:1) but wants to give us permanent inner peace every time an emotional issue comes up in our daily lives ("not yet"—Philippians 4:6,7). In addition, God has "already" justified believers' sins (taken away our guilty verdict) through Jesus' death, but he has "not yet" taken away our sinful natures, against which we still struggle (Romans 7:7-25).

For more instances of the "already/not-yet" aspects of the good news, read Ephesians 1-3 (statements) and then chapters 4-6 (commands). Other examples are Colossians 1-2 and 3-4 as well as Romans 1-11 and 12-16. Also, look at Hebrews 1-11 and 12-13.

Both inspired concepts are true. God has already accomplished our salvation, but it is also true that he continues to work it out in our lives, as the Holy Spirit enables us to cooperate with him (Philippians 2:12-13). I hope that this biblical distinction (learned from Dr. Andrew Bandstra, retired professor of Calvin Theological Seminary) helps you keep straight different biblical teachings in your mind.

Of course, the "not-yet" teachings of Scripture give us great hope for our future as believers. That hope is not unfounded "pie-in-the-sky." It is based on the firm historical foundation of Jesus' bodily resurrection, which clearly confirms the prediction of our future bodily resurrection.

Another passage which presents our hope is 2 Corinthians 5:1-5. [1] For we know that if the earthly tent we live in is destroyed, we have a building from God, an eternal house in heaven, not built by human hands. 2 Meanwhile we groan, longing to be clothed instead with our heavenly dwelling, 3 because when we are clothed, we will not be found naked. 4 For while we are in this tent, we groan and are burdened, because we do not wish to be unclothed but to be clothed instead with our heavenly dwelling, so that what is mortal may be swallowed up by life. 5 Now the one who has fashioned us for this very purpose is God, who has given us the Spirit as a deposit, guaranteeing what is to come. The Apostle Paul's inspired presentation shows us a lot of the following ideas about our hope:

(1) A lot of Christians believe that when we die, we will escape into heaven with only our souls, not our bodies. One question about this passage is whether the "building from God" in verse 1 is a completely-separate perfection of our souls or if it's our present bodies perfected.

(2) The answer, as always, depends on the verses surrounding this passage. Since verse one starts with "for" and since the chapter divisions are present for our convenience, we know that the previous verses are the basis for this verse. In chapter 4:14, Paul writes that since God has raised Jesus from the dead, he

will also raise us and welcome us into his presence, as he already does now through our prayers (see also Colossians 3:1-4).

(3) Therefore, our present earthly tent (our physical body) and our "eternal house" (verse 1) and "heavenly dwelling" are different and yet the same. They are the same body since God will raise us from death to life, not a different person (see Paul's references to seeds and plants in 1 Corinthians 15:35-41).

(4) Paul's "tent" and "house" are different in the same way that seeds are different from the plants that they produce. Again, refer to the passage I just mentioned in (3).

(5) God will build our heavenly dwelling, our resurrection body. Obviously, it will be perfect like Adam and Eve's bodies before their rebellion. It will also be full of the brilliant brightness of God and will last forever. It will experience no more pain or death. Come soon, Jesus!

(6) Coupled with our hope is groaning in the present for that great day when Jesus will raise us from the dead. We groan in the

present, but we cry tears combined with hope for our resurrection (verses 2 and 4).

(7) In verse 3, Paul writes that we are naked in our present body producing shame, just as our first parents have hidden themselves with leaves when they have shamefully decided to disobey God.

(8) However, God has given all true believers the Holy Spirit as his down payment on our future inheritances of a perfect body and universe—both full of God's glory.

Bible discussion questions:

(1) What do Christians generally think will happen to them after their deaths? Unbelievers? Explain.

(2) What do you think will happen to you after your death? Why?

(3) According the author, why did Paul write 1 Thessalonians 4:13-18? How do these verses comfort you about death? Explain.

(4) Read Matthew 5:1-10, especially verses 3,4, and 8, as well as the author's

explanations. What has impressed you about these three verses and the author's comments? Why?

(5) Explain in your own words the "already/not-yet" of the Bible's good news. Give an example from the Bible. In what way does that teaching help you understand the Scriptures better?

(6) Read 2 Corinthians 5:1-5. Which explanation of the author helps you the most for your Christian walk with Jesus? Why?

(7) Using the passages referred to in this section, what qualities will your resurrection body have? How do you feel about the future now that you have studied those verses? Why?

* * *

<u>One Step on our Journey with Jesus:</u> Spend time in your private prayer place praising God through Jesus by the Holy Spirit for his astounding plan to rescue believers from the human rebellion. Praise him for the certainty of his future plan to raise true Christians from death to eternal

life with our bright resurrection bodies for life in his new creation. Praise him for creating all humans and providing deliverance for some. Pray for people you know who show no evidence of being believers that God will rescue them before it's too late for them. Make plans to reach out to such neighbors and co-workers to be a friend to one or two of them. Pray for opportunities to share with them what God has done in your life.

* * *

<u>*Refreshment Station Eight*</u>—Do a different kind of praying.

Two kinds of complaining in the Bible
People have said to me, "You shouldn't ask God 'why?'" I have replied, "That's true if you're asking in total unbelief but not if you're asking in faith."

Two kinds of complaining appear in the Bible as follows:

Complaining in unbelief

We've already seen one of the kinds of complaining, which comes from unbelief and is usually directed at other people.

Every time the Israelites complain about the lack of food or water, the writer, Moses, clearly says that they grumble against him. In fact, God says to Moses at one point that his people have rebelled ten times in the desert. As a result, that whole generation, except for a few faithful followers, must die before the people can enter the Promised Land.

Even years after God provides the miraculous, heavenly bread, manna, they complain about that "miserable food." The LORD is our only real satisfaction in life, as Jesus teaches us when he identifies himself as God in his saying, "I am the bread of life." However, unbelieving grumbling doesn't look to him for its needs.

If they have been believers, they would have humbly shared their hunger with their focus on God in prayer for their "daily bread," as Jesus teaches us in the Lord's Prayer, Matthew 6:11.

I've seen a lot of professing Christians who let little irritations about their churches build up over the years. Then, some event happens to make them change churches. The problem is that they carry their dissatisfaction to the new church because it's never resolved. The same problem happens when a person leaves one relationship without dealing with the feelings of the first one.

One person said to me after she moved from one church to another that her anger began with words to which she and her husband objected twenty years previously and increased with each new irritation until the breaking point. I asked her if she ever shared her feelings with God or the church. She replied that she hadn't.

Complaining in genuine belief
Again, believing complaining is foreign to western cultures for some reason. Perhaps, in colder climates, we learned to keep our problems to ourselves, or the British "stiff upper lip" was very influential.

Whatever the reason, biblical examples of complaining in true faith abound in Scripture. In approaching these passages, we must not be like one TV preacher I heard. He called King David a "wimp" for complaining to God in the Psalms, where almost half of them have some complaining verses.

Instead, we need to take this pattern seriously for our own spiritual and mental health, as I've already written.

The book of Job

The book of Job is very instructive for us. In chapter 1:2, the Bible describes him as "blameless and upright." The first adjective means fully committed to God without outward blemish like the animals that were slaughtered as Israel's sacrifices. The word does not mean "perfect," the way older translations translated it.

In chapter 2, Job expresses his faith to his angry wife, who tells him to "curse God and die." Basically, he says that we should accept evil as well as good from God. Of course, he doesn't know that all his horrible losses come directly from Satan with God's required limits.

In the next chapter, his complaint in belief starts with the writer's description that he

curses the day of his birth (3:1). At length in
the whole chapter, Job wishes that God has
not given him life. Instead, he prefers to have
been stillborn by dying before his first
birthday.

Then, this blameless and upright man unloads
his anger on God, who can take it. Job's three
"friends" can't endure Job's lamenting but
blame him for some great sin that they think
must have brought on his suffering.

Again, in chapter 7:7-11, Job makes his
complaint to God clear:
7 Remember, O God, that my life is but a breath;
my eyes will never see happiness again.
8 The eye that now sees me will see me no longer;
you will look for me, but I will be no more.
9 As a cloud vanishes and is gone,
so one who goes down to the grave does not return.
10 He will never come to his house again;
his place will know him no more.
11 "Therefore I will not keep silent;
I will speak out in the anguish of my spirit,
I will complain in the bitterness of my soul.

If you and I had lost all ten of our children
and our whole wealth and health, we would
feel the same strong intensity of anger
("anguish" and "bitterness") as Job. Notice

that he expresses his feelings openly and honestly to God in lamenting prayer (verse 11).

Of course, his friends want to pin the cause of Job's suffering on him. He has the same faulty theology as they do, but he knows that he has committed no major sins to cause his huge suffering. That fact is his dilemma and the source of his complaints.

On the other hand, Jesus never points his finger of blame at people but instead looks at the larger picture as in John 11, where his followers ask him about the sinful cause of the blindness of a man who has been blind since his birth. Instead, Jesus says that it is for God's glory or honor. Then, he proceeds to heal the man, who proclaims his new faith in Jesus to the people who would later sentence Jesus to death.

In Job 7:7-11, Job complains about the meaninglessness and shortness of his life. He sounds depressed to me, but his breakthrough is verse 11, when he begins to express his angry complaint directly to God in his "friends'" presence.

Notice that contradicting Job's observation that no one who dies will come back to life, Jesus defies all human reasoning and experience to do just that miracle in order to give us hope for our future.

Like many humans, Job practices pragmatism, a philosophy that depends on our experiences to guide our lives. Much of the Bible is beyond human experiences, a reason why many people doubt it. Reliable eyewitnesses have written it down, but people's unbelieving pragmatism rejects it.

In chapter 23:1-6, Job imagines himself in the divine Judge's courtroom pleading his case,

1 Then Job replied:
2 "Even today my complaint is bitter;
his hand is heavy in spite of my groaning.
3 If only I knew where to find him;
if only I could go to his dwelling!
4 I would state my case before him
and fill my mouth with arguments.
5 I would find out what he would answer me,
and consider what he would say to me.
6 Would he vigorously oppose me?
No, he would not press charges against me.

Interestingly, Job is right that God has declared him "not guilty" but not because he

has avoided great sins. The reason is that God
the Father accepts Jesus' future suffering and
substitution for him on two crossed wooden
planks. That suffering in all believers' place
has been much greater than Job's and any of
the human struggles we might experience.

Job continues his complaint against God in
23:13-17,
13 "But he stands alone, and who can oppose him?
He does whatever he pleases.
14 He carries out his decree against me,
and many such plans he still has in store.
15 That is why I am terrified before him;
when I think of all this, I fear him.
16 God has made my heart faint;
the Almighty has terrified me.
17 Yet I am not silenced by the darkness,
by the thick darkness that covers my face.

He acknowledges God's unlimited power in
guiding human life, even God's inclusion of
Job's extreme suffering in his loving plan.

In verse 15, he admits his terror of God's
great power. However, he also fears God.
What's the difference? It's the same contrast
that Moses shares in Exodus 20:20 with
Israel's leaders after God shows his great
power on Mount Sinai by speaking the Ten

Commandments with his own voice. Moses says to them, "Do not be afraid. God has come to test you, so that the fear of God will be with you to keep you from sinning." The first fear is unbelieving terror of God, whereas the second is a believing respect for God's vast ability to run the universe and humans' lives.

Israel wants God to speak to Moses, who will then be his spokesperson. Their terror prevents them from experiencing the closeness with God that he has brought about by sending the second Person of God to earth in Jesus. Howver, Moses had that experience through God's gift of faith.

Anyway, Job's spiritual health shows up when he says in verse 17 that he refuses to be silent in God's powerful presence. He will express his intense feelings in honest laments.

In one more chapter (19), Job complains that other people as well as his "friends" pursue him like God with their condemnation. However, in the middle of his extreme anguish, he declares,

25 I know that my redeemer lives,
and that in the end he will stand on the earth.

26 And after my skin has been destroyed,
yet in my flesh I will see God;
27 I myself will see him
with my own eyes—I, and not another.
How my heart yearns within me!

This passage of great faith might surprise us, but Job's expressions of faith and complaint alternate in the book. These verses are difficult to translate from Hebrew into English, but a few truths are clear:

(1) Job has put his faith and trust in his "redeemer," whose life will rescue him. The law provides Israel with relief for defenseless widows in God's requirement that the closest relative must marry her to protect her from the dangers of extreme poverty. That extended family member is a "kinsman redeemer."

(2) Job feels like such a widow and senses that God has given him such a redeemer, to be fulfilled in Jesus' first coming.

(3) He also professes faith in God's presence with him after his death and along with his future resurrection (verses 26-27).

(4) Finally, in verse 27b, Job expresses his eager expectation of seeing God. All true believers have such feelings of faith for the future. Revelation 22 gives us that same promise.

How do we know that God accepts Job's believing complaints? In chapter 40:7, God says to Job's so-called friend Eliphaz, "I am angry with you and your two friends, because you have not spoken the truth about me, as my servant Job has." Thus, God requires them to sacrifice animals and get Job's approval as their priest.

Therefore, because of God's approval of a prayer pattern to which many people in western cultures are blind, he will also accept our tearful laments and heal our memories of the events causing our anger.

One more example should satisfy our interest in and expression of this unusual form of prayer, the book of Habakkuk. He is a prophet in southern Judah. Because he sees the extreme evil in Judah's conduct, he asks God why he allows it (1:2-3),

2 "How long, LORD, must I call for help,
but you do not listen?

Or cry out to you, 'Violence!'
but you do not save?
3 Why do you make me look at injustice?
Why do you tolerate wrongdoing?
Destruction and violence are before me;
there is strife, and conflict abounds."

We might ask God the same questions today. Sometimes, we mistake God's silence for indifference. However, God answers Habakkuk in 1:5-11 that he is going to send the powerful, wicked, ruthless Babylonians to punish Judah for their wickedness.

Habakkuk's next complaint is in 2:12-17. Basically, he asks God why he will use a people who are more immoral than the Judahites to deliver his judgment.

God responds in the rest of chapter two that he will also punish the Babylonians for their arrogant greed. He will fulfill that prophecy later when the Persians under King Cyrus overcome Babylon without one death or battle. The result is Cyrus' return of the Jews to their homeland.

In addition to Habakkuk's questioning laments, he expresses his amazing faith in

God's unlimited power at the end of this remarkable, short book,

17 Though the fig tree does not bud
and there are no grapes on the vines,
though the olive crop fails
and the fields produce no food,
though there are no sheep in the pen
and no cattle in the stalls,
18 yet I will rejoice in the LORD,
I will be joyful in God my Savior.
19 The Sovereign LORD is my strength;
he makes my feet like the feet of a deer,
he enables me to tread on the heights.

Habakkuk is no pragmatist, since his joyful faith in God is separate from his experiences of the struggles and losses of life.

One time I was teaching a church school class of high school students. I said that we believers cannot depend on our experiences as the basis for our faith in God. One of the students said, "Why not?" Another student replied, "When we experience losses in life, we can't depend on our experiences then, or our faith will fail." I said, "That's exactly right. We can, however, depend on God's Word, the Bible, to give us the truth about him."

<u>**Bible discussion questions:**</u>

(1) Which of you believe that we should never ask God "why?" Which of you believe that we should ask such a question if we feel it? Why or why not?

(2) Find a passage in Exodus or Numbers that describes Israel's grumbling. Ask everyone to turn to it. What is wrong with the people's complaining? What is God's punishment during the following forty years? Why? What role did Moses play in those events? What similar role can we play for people today? Explain.

(3) In the book of Job, chapters 1 and 2, which verses show Job's genuine, committed faith in God in the middle of his severe losses? Which verses show that God has the final authority over Satan? How do you feel about that truth? Why?

(4) In your own words, summarize Job's complaint in chapters 3; 7; and 23:13-17. How do his friends respond? What wrong idea about the cause of severe suffering do all of them have? Explain.

(5) On whose side in the disagreement between Job and his friends is God (see 40:7)? Why?

(6) In Habakkuk 1 and 2, summarize the questions that Habakkuk asks God as well as God's responses. What is Habakkuk's expression of faith in the middle of life's losses? How can we have such faith?

(7) Read a Psalm of personal lament (6, 22, 39, 42-43, or 88). What or who is the focus of that psalm? What makes it a song of faith? Why?

(8) How much do you agree with the charge that David is a wimp? Explain why you feel that way?

(9) What keeps Christians from expressing tearful laments in prayer? Why?

* * *

<u>One Step on our Journey with Jesus</u>: If you can't lament about your past disappointments concerning people's unloving actions and words for whatever

reason, find someone you trust (a pastor, counselor, or therapist) who will help you uncover your hidden hurts. Then, begin asking God your questions and expressing your honest emotions about your memories. Persist in your lamenting prayers. Continue this marathon in the meantime.

* * *

Refreshment Station Nine—Persist in praying.

Personal experiences

If you didn't get bogged down in examining your life during the previous leg of your marathon, the question arises, how many times do I need to pray laments to gain God's promised peace?

The short answer is "as many as it takes."

The long answer is that since we can fall victim to our culture's "fast-food" mentality, we become impatient with any process that takes a long time.

My personal experiences with laments may be helpful to you. After forty-three years of unconscious anger and anxiety, I lamented for a marathon of ight and a half months three or four times a week before God gave me the inner emotional peace of Philippians 4:7, which has lasted more than three decades at this point.

I have experienced at least three kinds of chronic pain for more than three decades also. More than twenty years ago, God made me realize that I was angry about it because I was getting depression-weary again. That time, I lamented sixty times every night for two months until God gave me that same peace, which continues to this day.

In addition, I had seven years of daily migraines of varying intensity. I lamented many times until God provided his peace about that issue.

By the way, God completely took away my seven-year depression and daily migraines but allowed my pain to remain as my "thorn in the flesh" like Paul's (2 Corinthians 12:1-10). However, in every experience with lamenting, God has enabled me to accept the sources of my anger and anxiety, which decreased dramatically in intensity.

You might be interested in knowing what that peace has been like. First, it means an acceptance of the presence of the events, losses, and afflictions in my life. Second, it means that I have given to God, the perfect Judge, the unloving actions of other people for him to judge. Third, since my anger has decreased from great intensity to minor irritation, I have changed from living with huge stress in my body's muscles to being "laid-back," in the words of a janitor in one of my churches. These results are all God's wonderful gifts.

Therefore, my strong recommendation is that you keep on lamenting until God gives you his permanent peace at the end of our marathon. You can see that God also blesses such prayers with health benefits.

Examples in the Bible of persistent prayers

Old Testament passages about prayer
Now we turn to Genesis 32:22-32 as one example of persistent prayer. Jacob is very scared because his estranged brother, Esau, is

approaching with four hundred men. He puts his whole family across a stream and camps alone that night. A mysterious man wrestles with him. Jacob persistently holds his own all night. Then, the man merely dislocates his hip by touching it.

However, Jacob holds onto the man, literally for dear life. The man wants to leave at daybreak, but Jacob says that he will not let go of him unless the man blesses him. As a result, the man gives him the name Israel because of his persistence in wrestling and praying.

Israel asks the man's name, but he blesses Jacob instead. Israel realizes who has wrestled with him in naming the stream beside which he has camped Peniel, which means "face of God."

A reasonable interpretation is that the second Person of God—later to become Jesus—took human form to teach Jacob and us the value of persistent prayer and to bless him as a result.

Furthermore, God foretells Israel's rebellion in and exit from the Promised Land. Hundreds of years before it happens, in Moses' message in Deuteronomy 4:29-30, the LORD promises Jacob's descendants, "But if from there you seek the LORD your God, you will find him if you seek him with all your heart and with all your soul. When you are in distress and all these things have happened to you, then in later days you will return to the LORD your God and obey him."

Notice that it's not just persistent prayers that God wants, but he also desires sincere, fervent, genuine prayers, not just scripted, monotonous, traditional prayers that we hardly mean. We must put our whole being into those prayers—our minds, feelings, and wills.

New Testament passages about prayer
Moreover, at the end of Luke's version of Jesus' teaching on prayer, Jesus provides the punchline in Luke 11:13, "If you then, though you are evil, know how to give good gifts to your children, how much more will your Father in heaven give the Holy Spirit to those who ask him!"

Notice here Jesus' teaching that our Father wants to give us good gifts much more than our earthly fathers. The best Gift is the Holy Spirit, who is the direct Source of inner peace. Of course, God won't give us gifts that are out of his will, but we should already know that he wants the Holy Spirit to give us inner peace, as he has promised. Our Father wants to give it to us through Jesus' victory by the Spirit's power. Therefore, we need to persist in asking him for it with our laments.

Probably the most direct passage of Jesus' teaching on persistent prayer is Luke 18:1-8. In verse one, Luke gives away the meaning of Jesus' parable, "Then Jesus told his disciples a parable to show them that they should always pray and not give up." Then, he tells them the story of an unjustly treated widow who relentlessly visits an unbelieving and corrupt judge to get justice.

Finally, the unjust judge gives in because of her persistence. Jesus concludes in verses 7 and 8, "And will not God bring about justice for his chosen ones, who cry out to him day and night? Will he keep putting them off? I tell you, he will see that they get justice, and quickly. However, when the Son of Man comes, will he find faith on the earth?" If we are convinced that some request is God's will, we need to pray persistently. He is our willing heavenly Father.

However, I have one word of caution. We may pray fervently and persistently for someone's healing from a terminal illness, but that person dies. Our experience doesn't seem to agree with Jesus' teachings and may make us doubt.

Hold on a minute. When believers die, their healing begins then and is completed when they are resurrected. God doesn't always answer our prayers the exact way we want him to. We must not be like the dog's tail trying to wag its owner!

On the other hand, God does want to give us inner, emotional peace in this life (Philippians 4:6-7) as a foretaste of perfectly-complete and constant peace in our next life. Thus, we can confidently and persistently pray for it, while expressing our feelings honestly.

Two other brief verses are commands for persistent prayers. Romans 12:12 says, "Be joyful in hope, patient in affliction, faithful in prayer." After Paul's descriptions of humanity's guilt (chapters 1:1—3:20) and

God's great grace to believers (3:21—11:36), he calls true Christians in his remaining chapters to act on God's rescue, while relying on his power.

He calls us to be "faithful in prayer." Satan wants to lure us away from praying by using the busyness of life or our disappointments. On the other hand, Jesus wants us to persist in our prayers, as we've seen. Who do you suppose we should follow?

You see why it's very important to have a private, personal, prayer place where we read the Scriptures and pray our personal prayers.

The other Bible verse is 1 Thessalonians 5:17 between verses in which Paul calls us to constant joy and thanks. He writes, "Pray continually." The original word means "all the time." How more persistent can we get?!

We also might ask the following question: How can I pray all the time? First, God owns our time; we don't. Second, since he owns our time and we are in his presence constantly, he wants to have a constant conversation. Third, before some activity during which we need to concentrate, we can pray for his blessing.

Fourth, afterwards, we can thank him for his blessing or pray for the lessons we need to learn from our mistakes. Fifth, when our minds pray to him, he doesn't often give us immediate answers. Sixth, those answers often enter our minds as ideas at some other times when we need them. Seventh, we don't need to expect audible voices or visions, though God sometimes gives them.

The important teaching to remember and put into practice is that God wants our time dedicated to him for a constant dialogue with him, while we also need to set aside time daily to pray privately.

Many Christians are also familiar with Ephesians 6:10-17, in which Paul calls us to put on God's powerful armor like the equipment of Roman soldiers in order to be Jesus' soldier.

However, fewer people are aware that he continues with a word about prayer (verse 18), "And pray in the Spirit on all occasions with all kinds of prayers and requests. With this in mind, be alert and always keep on praying for all the Lord's people."

This verse is directly connected in the original language to the previous verses about God's armor represented in this translation by the word "and." In other words, believers' prayers are essential for their own personal ongoing victory and the church's triumph resulting in God's gift of spiritual and numerical growth. Furthermore, our prayers are like the straps that has held the Roman soldier's equipment together. When we stop praying, Satan can attack and influence us.

Our Internet just went out. It is the connection between my computer and other computers all over the world, as you probably already know. However, God's personal knowledge about us and every person in the world is complete. He never stops to take a break or to sleep but continues all the time to work every action and event out for the good of his people (Romans 8:28). His listening ear is always ready to hear and act on our prayers according to his perfect will.

By the way, our Internet just came back on after I unplugged and plugged in our provider's modem. However, God doesn't need rebooting!

Sometimes life can seem overwhelming. The Apostle John has some teaching to help us when struggles come. In 1 John 5:1-5, he describes for us God's gift of our biblical self-image, "1 Everyone who believes that Jesus is the Christ is born of God, and everyone who loves the father loves his child as well. 2 This is how we know that we love the children of God: by loving God and carrying out his commands. 3 In fact, this is love for God: to keep his commands. And his commands are not burdensome, 4 for everyone born of God overcomes the world. This is the victory that has overcome the world, even our faith. 5 Who is it that overcomes the world? Only the one who believes that Jesus is the Son of God." Then, in verses 14-15, he writes these inspired words, "14 This is the confidence we have in approaching God: that if we ask anything according to his will, he hears us. 15 And if we know that he hears us—whatever we ask—we know that we have what we asked of him." Note the following observations:

(1) John was the follower of Jesus who was especially close to him, having been described as the one Jesus loved. Here, he says that we must believe in Jesus' Messiahship, that is, his divine-human right to rule the universe and our lives. If we do have such faith, God has given us the miracle of his new birth (verse 1a).

(2) The evidence of our new birth is love for other children of God (verse 1b). Of course, love is a commitment of our wills to do good for other Christians regardless of their imperfections, which we all have. Obviously, we can't fulfill this kind of love by staying away from church.

(3) Such horizontal love starts with our vertical relationship with God (verses 2-3). Some people think that only the Old Testament has God's commands and that the New Testament is all about his love. Well, John's teaching makes it clear that God's Old and New Testament commands apply to us. Following them demonstrates our loving commitment to our Rescuer and Ruler.

(4) What is the Christian self-image? Is it self-improvement in our own strength like a lot of New Year's resolutions? We just passed another January 1. What percentage of people's resolutions will become permanent? The successful self-image is that we are God's overcomers by the unlimited power of Jesus' victory.

(5) John says as much. God's free gifts of faith in Jesus as God's unique Son and the new birth enable us to overcome the world's evil temptations (verses 4-5).

(6) In verses 14-15, John says that the key to sharing in Jesus' triumph is prayer. He qualifies the prayers that we ask by saying that they must be "according to his will." Therefore, prayer is not a blank check on which we can write anything that we selfishly want. Jesus reserves the right to make the final decision.

(7) The reason God does not answer "yes" to every prayer is that he sees and guides the larger picture of our lives, whereas we have a limited view of our lives and other people's lives. Besides, we often ask him with selfish motives (see James 4:1-3).

(8) However, if God's Word clearly teaches his will about anything, we can be confident that when our prayers are consistent with that teaching, he will answer our prayers "yes." The answer may take years to happen, but it will, perhaps after we've gone to be with him.

Now, we need some humor about prayer (jokes.christiansunite.com).

* * *

As the storm raged, the captain realized his ship was sinking fast. He called out, "Anyone here know how to pray?" One man stepped forward. "Aye, Captain, I know how to pray."

"Good," said the captain, "you pray while the rest of us put on our life jackets - we're one short."

* * *

Johnny, a very bright 5-year-old, told his daddy he'd like to have a baby brother and, along with his request, offered to do whatever he could to help. His dad, a very bright 35-year-old, paused for a moment and then replied, " I'll tell you what, Johnny, if you pray every day for two months for a baby brother, I guarantee that God will give you one!"

Johnny responded eagerly to his dad's challenge and went to his bedroom early that night to start praying for a baby brother.

He prayed every night for a whole month, but after that time, he began to get skeptical. He checked around the neighborhood and found out that what he thought was going to happen, had never occurred in the history of the neighborhood. You just don't pray for two months and then, whammo- a new baby

brother. So, Johnny quit praying. After another
month, Johnny's mother went to the hospital. When
she came back home, Johnny's parents called him into
the bedroom. He cautiously walked into the room, not
expecting to find anything, and there was a little
bundle lying right next to his mother. His dad pulled
back the blanket and there was -- not one baby
brother, but two!! His mother had twins!

Johnny's dad looked down at him and said, "Now
aren't you glad you prayed?"

Johnny hesitated a little and then looked up at his
dad and said, "Yes, but aren't you glad I quit when I
did?"

Bible discussion questions:

(1) What is your response to the two jokes at
the end of this section? Why do you react that
way?

(2) What keeps Christians from being
persistent in praying for something that we
know God wants? Explain.

(3) Read Genesis 32:22-32 and Deuteronomy
4:29-30. What qualities of prayer do both of
these passages, taken together, call us to
have? Why?

(4) Read Luke 11:13 and 18:1-8. Tell in your own words how the meanings of these two passages relate? What do they mean for your life?

(5) Read Romans 12:12 and 1 Thessalonians 5:17 in their contexts. How can we obey these commands about prayer, practically speaking?

(6) Read Ephesians 6:10-20. Explain in your own words Paul's teaching about the armor and how it relates to verses 18 and 19, which deal with prayer. Based on these verses, how can we be more effective in our prayer life?

(7) Read 1 John 5:1-5, 14-15. According to this passage, why isn't prayer a "blank check" getting us anything we want? Which ones of the author's comments help you the most? Explain.

* * *

<u>One Step on our Journey with Jesus</u>: List on a sheet of paper or your electronic device the lessons you learned from this section about the best qualities of prayer. Pray for each one that you need to develop until God gives you more of it. Also, pray

to overcome the qualities that you need to overcome and to gain the biblical qualities. Remember, persist in prayer by claiming Jesus' all-powerful victory.

* * *

Life's Emotional Marathon Part IV

Refreshment Station 10—Praise God for his permanent peace.

We have now come to the last refreshment station before the finish line. Take as long as it takes to complete this last leg of the marathon as you persist in prayer.

While you struggle to complete this rugged marathon, the Holy Spirit wants to continue feeding you with his inspired Word from the Father through Jesus to give you enough energy to complete the race.

We turn to Matthew 11:20-30. In verses 20-24, Jesus condemns the towns who have rejected him. Then, we find his words for his faithful ones: 25 At that time Jesus said, "I praise you, Father, Lord of heaven and earth, because you have hidden these things from the wise and learned and revealed them to little children. 26 Yes, Father, for this is what you were pleased to do. 27 All things have been committed to me by my Father. No one knows the Son except the Father, and no one knows the Father except the Son and those to whom the Son chooses to reveal him. 28 Come to me, all you who are weary and burdened, and I will give you rest. 29 Take my yoke upon you and learn from me, for I am gentle and humble in heart, and you will find rest for your souls. 30 For my yoke is easy and my burden is light." These verses prompt several observations:

(1) Notice how Jesus addresses his Father as the Lord or Ruler of the universe. This prayer brings up an important teaching about the relationship between Jesus and his Father, who are both fully God along with the Holy Spirit. Therefore, the three Persons have equal status within God.

(2) However, even though the oneness of the three Persons is clear, they play different roles or functions. The Father is the Source; the Son, the Agent; and the Holy Spirit, the Atmospheric-Person who is the direct Cause of the one God's work. That distinction between their oneness and their different

functions is important, since two dangers exist in people's minds.

(3) One danger is to think that God is one Person, while the other is to think that he is three separate Gods. The church has rightly rejected both extremes because they are ways to reason one's way out of the profound mystery that is clearly taught in Scripture that God is three Persons in one God. We need to accept that mystery because the Bible teaches it. After all, who am I as a mere creature to figure out and completely understand my all-powerful Creator?

(4) In verses 25-26, Jesus praises God the Father because he is the original Source of humans' creation, rescue, and restoration. Of course, Jesus is the Agent of those actions, while the Holy Spirit is the Atmosphere making all of them directly possible. Two examples are the Holy Spirit's hovering over the chaos before God begins to give order to the creation (Genesis 1:2b) and over Mary's womb to join the Second Person with her humanity (Matthew 1:20b).

(5) Anyway, Jesus praises the Father for hiding the truth about Jesus from the highly educated and giving it to ordinary people like the tax collector and fishermen among his closest followers.

(6) His praise points up God's unlimited power to reveal and not reveal truths to anyone he wishes. Of course, at the same time, most of the self-important religious leaders have hardened hearts because their pride has made them think who the Messiah will be. Jesus doesn't fit their mold.

(7) Both truths are biblical: God rules every creature in his universe and among his people. At the same time, humans are fully responsible for all that they do, think, and feel. Now, you have another biblical mystery that we can leave up to God to solve.

(8) Verse 27 points to another amazing truth about the relationship between the Father and Jesus. They "know" each other intimately. Of course, Jesus doesn't mean sexually because the Father doesn't have a physical body unlike the false god imagined by some religious groups. He is "spirit," not flesh and

blood (John 4:24). The word "know," when it describes the relationship between persons means the commitment of loving action. For instance, when Paul writes that God has foreknown us before he made the universe, he means that God fore-loved us (Romans 8:29).

(9) Therefore, on the basis of these astounding truths, Jesus calls us to come to him for "rest." God has promised Israel rest from the enemies around and in the promised land if they would only obey his law. However, they forget much of it and stubbornly depart from God's good guidelines in order to worship the false gods of the Canaanites and other ones.

(10) The "yoke" is the carved piece of wood that usually stretches across two animals. The yoke enables the oxen or other animals to pull a plow that prepares the soil for planting or a cart to carry items. Jesus says if we carry around with us heavy emotional burdens, we need to come to him for his yoke. He will be the other one to help us carry a much lighter burden with his lighter yoke because he pulls it with us.

(11) He says that we must learn from him, which is the reason we must read and listen to

his Word. His call is the reason we need teachers and preachers outside of us so that we stay on Jesus' way to our heavenly Father.

(12) One other detail is important. Jesus describes himself as "gentle and humble in heart." Gentleness, which other passages recommend for our lives, is not being a doormat. Rather, it is asserting our ideas and emotions and then submitting to other people's and God's decisions. Jesus shows this trait at his kangaroo-court trial when he asserts that he is God and then submits to the authorities' decision to kill him. Humility is the characteristic of recognizing and accepting our low position in life. Jesus shows it when he prays to his heavenly Father, since his position and role as the God-man are lower in honor than his Father's on the throne of the universe.

The next passage with which God wants to refresh us on the last leg of our marathon is Philippians 3:10-14: 10 "I want to know Christ— yes, to know the power of his resurrection and participation in his sufferings, becoming like him in his death, 11 and so, somehow, attaining to the resurrection from the dead. 12 Not that I have already obtained all this, or have already arrived at my goal, but I press on to take hold of that for which Christ Jesus took hold of me. ¹³ Brothers and sisters, I do not consider myself yet to have taken hold of it. But one thing I do: Forgetting what is behind and straining toward what is ahead, ¹⁴ I press on toward the goal to win the prize for which God has called me heavenward in Christ Jesus." Consider the following thoughts:

(1) In the first nine verses of Philippians 3, the Apostle Paul describes all his self-righteous qualities on which he has relied before he has become a Christian. His pedigree has been without a flaw. If people can get into heaven on their merits, he certainly can. However, he meets Jesus on the road to Damascus. As a result of that powerful meeting, all his self-reliance and pride are now gone.

(2) Now, his only focus is Jesus (verse 10). The background to this passage is the Greek Olympics and running a race. Paul's goal at the finish line is resurrection perfection. Our goal during this marathon is Jesus' gift of the permanent peace that only he can give us.

(3) Paul starts out by saying that he wants to know or personally love Christ. Of course, he already knows Christ, but he wants to

experience that personal relationship more deeply.

(4) Notice the unusual content of this knowledge in verses 10b-11. Our deeper experience of Jesus must mirror Paul's. Knowing Jesus means taking part in his suffering and death. In what sense? This life is bound to bring us suffering of one kind or another, and it will inevitably bring us death unless Jesus comes first.

(5) Obviously, we can't suffer and die in exactly the same way Jesus does. Our flawless, sinless Substitute as the divine-human Son of the Father takes the path of unique suffering and death to remove our guilt. On the other hand, our suffering and death happen to flawed, sinful humans. However, in some sense, our suffering is part of his suffering. Think about that truth the next time you lose a close parent or relative.

(6) The result is that Jesus wants to go through such times of suffering with us since he has full sympathy for our grief, anger, and anxiety.

(7) The object of Paul's desire that needs to become our energetic motivation to finish the marathon is Jesus' resurrection power. The final, overall goal of our whole life s the "resurrection of the dead."

(8) However, Paul and we are not perfect yet (verse 12). Even when we reach the finish line of our marathon with Jesus' resurrection power, the result will be emotional peace about the issues leading up to the present. Other disappointments will arise, and we will need to lament or grieve those losses and irritants in another marathon. With Paul, we need to confess that we are not perfect yet. Thus, we always need to run the overall race toward our resurrection perfection, which will only come at our bodily resurrection. If Paul is not yet perfect, none of us can really claim to be perfect either.

(9) In verses 12-14, Paul uses the verbs "press" and "strain" that are also related to the Greeks running a race. In those verses, Paul again confesses that he is far from perfect. Apparently, some Philippians think that he has arrived at the perfection-line before his death and that they can too. The picture that he draws is urgent, fervent effort to win the

race. Of course, every true Christian will also win the race toward perfection, but that fact is no excuse to avoid making the effort to gain God's gift of growth toward that goal.

(10) In the Christian life, we have many marathons. This one is our present one striding toward the finish line of emotional peace about our past, but we also must seek his peace for other issues concerning our deciding and thinking, for example. In our struggles toward resurrection perfection, we have to run many marathons until we reach the final finish line when we die or when Jesus returns.

The previous verses offend perfectionists. Another familiar passage offends people who think that all people will go to heaven (universalists), John 14:6. Jesus has been comforting his twelve followers because he has just said that he will be leaving them. Doubting Thomas says that he doesn't know where Jesus is going. Then, Jesus makes a controversial statement, "I am the way and the truth and the life. No one comes to the Father except through me."

For people I've met who say that all religions are different ways to the same final bliss, this verse is unacceptable. I've met three very-different people who have believed this idea of universalism—one of my high school English teachers, a Native American, and an eighty-year-old neighbor.

Contrary to all of them, Jesus says "I am." In this one of several "I am" statements in John's book, Jesus claims to be the God who appeared to Moses in the unburnable burning bush (Exodus 3 and 4) and who gave his name as I AM. Jesus also makes the bold statement that he is the Source of truth and life, both of which are themes that John emphasizes and connects with God.

His boldest claim is that he is the only way to God the Father. Everyone has two choices about Jesus at this point. Either he is mentally ill in claiming to be God, or he is God. He can't be only a good teacher or prophet. Through God's gift of faith in him, we trust that he is God because we take him at his word. He confirms his claim with his bodily resurrection.

For our marathon, not only is he our Guide, but he's also the Highway to heaven for our marathon. That fact shows us why our race is such a struggle uphill! It's also the reason we need to pray constantly for Jesus' all-powerful presence to give us his strength.

Colossians 3:15 is also Paul's command concerning our struggle to gain God's peace, "Let the peace of Christ rule in your hearts, since as members of one body you were called to peace. And be thankful." Not only does Jesus want us to have emotional peace, but we also have to let him give it to us. We need to confess any resistance we may feel to finishing the marathon and ask for fresh resolve. A great amount of thankfulness will result in our lives.

This verse also extends our inner peace to the body of Christians, the church. Our peace will affect other believers in the church of which we're a part. For example, if God lowers our anger and anxiety levels, other people will notice the difference and ask us. Then, we can testify to God's work in our lives. The result will be to build up other Christians in the faith.

Now, we come to one key passage upon which our marathon is based, Philippians 4:6-7, "Do not be anxious about anything, but in every situation, by prayer and petition, with thanksgiving, present your requests to God. And the peace of God, which transcends all understanding, will guard your hearts and your minds in Christ Jesus."

Paul gives us God's commands and his promise. The commands are not to be anxious but share all kinds of prayers with God, including thanks. The following list has the kinds of prayers that people make in the Bible:

> - Praise for God's actions in history and his divine qualities,
> - Thanks for his many undeserved blessings,
> - Confession of our many sins and imperfections,
> - Prayer for other people's needs,
> - Prayer for our needs,
> - Lament expressing genuine feelings about God's plans and other people's actions.

These prayers are the parts of people's prayers to which Paul is referring. I have emphasized lamenting because it is absent from the western culture, but I recommend to you all of these prayers for your marathon prayers until God gives you his gift of your inner peace at the finish line and afterwards.

Paul says that God's peace "transcends all understanding" because it often comes before our circumstances change. In fact, our situation may never be different, but we will come to accept those events that have disturbed us. In addition, the levels of our anger and anxiety will decrease dramatically.

It is for this reason that our marathon is very worthwhile, since God will change us for the better, emotionally.

One last observation is about verse 7. Paul also writes that God's peace will be like a military guard of our lives' forts by standing all the time in order to defend us against Satan's attacks.

In my experience of three decades with God's peace about issues about my first forty-three years, his peace persists. Also, his peace about more recent events about which I lamented has lasted to this day. Some people claim to have peace that comes and goes. However, his peace is a permanent guard over our lives as long as our lives are focused on God.

Bible discussion questions:

(1) Read Matthew 11:25-30. Take some time to read these verses over and over and to meditate on them in the light of the author's comments. What reactions do you have? What verse stands out in your mind? Why? Which one of the author's comments means the most for your life? Why?

(2) Notice that Matthew 11:25-26 records Jesus' prayer to our heavenly Father. What do you learn about the Father and Jesus in these verses? Our relationship to them? Explain each answer.

(3) Read Philippians 3:10-14. Why are these verses particularly relevant to our emotional marathon? Explain. Which ones of the author's observations mean the most for your daily life? Why?

(4) How does Jesus' claim in John 14:6 relate to our emotional marathon, according to the author? Why is Jesus' statement controversial? Explain. Why should we accept his claim?

(5) According to Colossians 3:15, what is the relationship between the peace that God gives us and that of the church of which we're a part? Why?

(6) Read Philippians 4:6-7. Why is this passage important for running our emotional marathon? Explain.

(7) Memorize and use the six kinds of prayers in your personal prayers. Which one is the most important to your Christian life now? Why?

(8) Why does God's peace "transcend" our understanding? How do we know that his peace is permanent, according to the author? Explain your answers.

* * *

<u>One Step on Our Journey with Jesus</u>: Take a week to read and meditate on your

desires to put each one of the verses in this section into practice. Ask God for Jesus' victory to turn them into action. Persist in your laments until you reach the emotional finish line of permanent peace about past issues. Then, praise God for his grace in giving you progress.

* * *

While you lope laboriously toward the finish line, let this very-relevant passage (Hebrews 12:1-8) and the following comments encourage you to complete this part of your life's emotional journey: Therefore, since we are surrounded by such a great cloud of witnesses, let us throw off everything that hinders and the sin that so easily entangles. And let us run with perseverance the race marked out for us, 2 fixing our eyes on Jesus, the pioneer and perfecter of faith. For the joy set before him he endured the cross, scorning its shame, and sat down at the right hand of the throne of God. 3 Consider him who endured such opposition from sinners, so that you will not grow weary and lose heart. 4 In your struggle against sin, you have not yet resisted to the point of shedding your blood. 5 And have you completely forgotten this word of encouragement that addresses you as a father addresses his son? It says, "My son, do not make light of the Lord's discipline, and do not lose heart when he rebukes you, 6 because the Lord disciplines the one he loves, and he chastens everyone he accepts as his son."

7 Endure hardship as discipline God is treating you as his children. For what children are not disciplined by their father? 8 If you are not disciplined—and everyone undergoes discipline—then you are not legitimate, not true sons and daughters at all.

(1) Verse 1 starts by referring to chapter 11, in which the writer lists a large number of Old Testament "heroes of faith," who are ordinary, weak people whom God empowers to overcome God's enemies and do great actions through faith. Those gifts from God are trust in him and hope for a better future.

(2) Those witnesses surround us as spectators who are watching and cheering us on to finish the marathon. Because of the encouragement we receive reading the previous chapter, the writer gives us two commands in the rest of verse one.

(3) Therefore, we are to throw away our galoshes of guilt and secret sins. In addition, we must run our race with continuing effort ("perseverance"). God has marked out our

emotional race with a great prize at the finish line, inner peace.

(4) Verses 2 and 3 give us great incentive to complete our marathon. The writer puts our focus where it should be, not on our own emotional exhaustion but on Jesus. He has gone ahead of us to pave our way by choosing to suffer in carrying our guilt, sins, and imperfections all the way to his death at the hands of the cruel, sadistic Romans. He is, indeed, the divine-human Hero, who rescues us.

(5) In verses 4-6, the inspired writer says that our struggles are God's loving discipline from the only perfect Father, not from an imperfect father that everyone of us had.

(6) In verses 7-8, he says that if we are genuinely adopted children of God, he will discipline us through the work of his Holy Spirit using his Word. When we are open to God's correction as we read the Bible and listen to preachers and teachers as well as other people within a small group, he is using the Bible as his disciplinary tool.

(7) If we are closed or have spiritual blind spots to our need for spiritual change, God may have to permit a major jolt in our lives to wake us up. Here, we must distinguish between God's permissive plan and Satan's attacks that directly bring about tragic or evil circumstances in our lives. God is never the direct cause of suffering, as the first two chapters of the book of Job show clearly.

IMPORTANT NOTE: God's gift of inner peace will be permanent ONLY as you continue to focus your life on him.

Finally, the last chapter of the Bible has a lot of encouragement for us. Revelation 22:1-5 pictures us as the new Jerusalem, symbolic of the final people of God, who will live with us on the new earth. All our marathons will be finished when Jesus returns: [1] Then the angel showed me the river of the water of life, as clear as crystal, flowing from the throne of God and of the Lamb [2] down the middle of the great street of the city. On each side of the river stood the tree of life, bearing twelve crops of fruit, yielding its fruit every month. And the leaves of the tree are for the healing of the nations. [3] No longer will there be any curse. The throne of God and of the Lamb will be in the city, and his servants will serve him. [4] They will see his face, and his name will be on their foreheads. [5]

There will be no more night. They will not need the light of a lamp or the light of the sun, for the Lord God will give them light. And they will reign for ever and ever.

(1) In verses 1-3, the city has the water (and tree) of life near it. God has provided water from a dry rock and manna when there is no bread for the Israelites in the desert. Moreover, Jesus claims to have living water (John 4) and be the bread of life (John 6). He is all we will need for life in the new universe that he will create out of this decaying one.

(2) Another obvious reference in these verses is to the garden of Eden's tree of life, from which rebellious humans cannot eat. However, perfected believers will have full access to that ever-giving "tree." Also, notice that the water of life comes from the throne of God the Father and God the Son (the "Lamb").

(3) The Apostle John's vision also involves an observation that the curse will disappear (verse 3a). Of course, all humans experience the struggles of God's curse of Genesis 3 because all of us have rebelled against him since Adam and Eve's disobedience. We have

brought diseases, disasters, death, and destruction on ourselves because we have turned to self-centered living. God is not at fault for any of them. We brought them on ourselves, and Satan is their immediate cause.

(4) Notice our careers in that new place of true believers; we "will serve him." In the next verse, we discover another clue to our activities in the new creation, we "will reign for ever and ever." Now you know as much as I do about our work there. However, we will have worthwhile actions to do throughout eternity, that is, taking care of the new universe, obviously under the rulership of God.

(5) In verse 4, we see a descriptive detail that God has forbidden now; then, we will "see his face." Remember that even Moses can only see God's "back" when he asks to see God in Exodus 34. I have no idea what seeing God's back means since he is spirit, not flesh and blood. Of course, Jesus' human body is now in heaven, but the Father doesn't have one.

(6) Can you imagine having no sun or artificial lighting? In verse 5, we notice that night will be no more and that we will live

forever in the bright light of God's glory always. I can't wait but will have to since God has given me mission to be his author!

(7) Our marathon's finish line will provide the great relief of inner peace, but it falls far short of the final relief that God will give us when he provides us with resurrection perfection. However, our emotional goal will be God's foretaste of that final day's complete and final victory.

Then, in verse 10, the angel gives John and us some advice that will be a result of our inner peace. He says, "Let the one who does wrong continue to do wrong; let the vile person continue to be vile; let the one who does right continue to do right; and let the holy person continue to be holy."

Why is this verse the result of the completion of our marathon? When God gives us peace as a dramatic decrease in our anger and anxiety, we will be ready to obey his words. The reason is that anger tries to control other people because of the anxious insecurity in their lives, but it won't control ours.

This verse says that we must let go of our attempts to control other people's actions and lifestyles. In other words, all people will answer to God for all their self-centered thoughts, words, and actions. They won't answer to us. God is by far the best Judge, not us.

Therefore, God commands us to let him be the Judge. Please don't take that job on yourself. For example, that sad result is what gossip does. Such talk puts people in a negative light without finding out their sides of the stories. Negative stories destroy people's reputation, a little like murder.

The reason we aren't supposed to be people's judges is found in verse 12, "Look, I am coming soon! My reward is with me, and I will give to each person according to what they have done. I am the Alpha and the Omega, the First and the Last, the Beginning and the End."

Jesus speaks these words claiming to be the eternal, divine Judge, who will call all people to account for their whole lives when he comes back. The three pairs of titles emphasize Jesus' eternal nature as God with the Father and the Holy Spirit.

Of course, all of us are imperfect and therefore unacceptable, unless God creates a new heart and faith in us. Then, because of Jesus' perfect life, death as our Substitute, and resurrection for our new birth, God the Father gives us his verdict of "not guilty" and welcomes us into the new Jerusalem.

Finally, in verse 20, "He who testifies to these things says, 'Yes, I am coming soon.'" How can we believe Jesus' words when it's been almost two millennia since John heard and wrote these words in about A.D. 90? The answer is that God's "soon" is different from ours, as several other passages say. We can't hold God to our puny ideas about time or anything else, for that matter.

Then, the Apostle John's words echo believers' hope since Adam and Eve and all humans messed up themselves and God's creation,

"Amen. Come, Lord Jesus."

As you break the tape at the finish line, thank God for your hope of the final, perfect peace that we will all experience at the end of time.

Bible discussion questions:

(1) Read Hebrews 12:1-8 after reviewing chapter 11. Which verses stand out to you in this passage? Why?

(2) Which one of the author's comments is most important to you in your running of your emotional marathon? Explain.

(3) If you have already reached the finish line with God's reward of inner peace, share your experience with your group. How has he changed your life? Explain.

(4) Who is responsible for tragedies and other evil events in our lives? Why? How is God involved?

(5) Read Revelation 22. Which verses help your Christian life the most? Why?

(6) Which one of the author's observations is the most helpful for your life right now? Explain.

(7) How does verse 10 apply to Christians' daily lives? How hard is letting God judge people instead of our judging or condemning them? How is our judging people different from our discerning good from evil? Explain.

(8) How will emotional peace affect the way we talk about other people? Explain.

* * *

<u>One Step on Our Journey with Jesus</u>: If you have already received God's reward of grace at the finish line, praise and thank him because it's all to his credit since he gave you the strength and the gift to gain it. At the same time, tell other people near you what God has done, always giving him the honor. If you haven't yet reached the finish line, please persevere to gain his promise of peace completely to his credit.

* * *

I give you the following blessing from the Apostle Paul:

Now may the Lord of peace himself give you peace at all times and in every way. The Lord be with all of you (1 Thessalonians 3:16).

Amen!!

www.ingramcontent.com/pod-product-compliance
Lightning Source LLC
Chambersburg PA
CBHW061513120726
48001CB00004B/1311